This innovative study, commissioned by Governor Mario Cuomo, examines the economic and environmental future of eastern Long Island, including the towns of Southampton, Riverhead, East Hampton, Southold, and Shelter Island. Developed as a paradigm for the interaction of a local community with state government, the report was approached with one goal in mind: to strengthen the East End economy without adversely affecting its environment.

The 49-member volunteer task force, the first of its kind in New York State history, included public officials, farmers, bank presidents, fishermen, environmentalists, motel and marina operators, vineyard and restaurant owners, and real estate brokers. After five months of intense work they made 44 specific recommendations covering the agricultural, fishing, winery, and recreation/second home industries, which are the backbone of the rural East End economy.

The complete report was delivered to the Governor on November 19, 1993. This is the only full-length publication of the report in book form.

The publication of this book was made possible through funding by the following organizations and individuals to whom the Task Force is most grateful:

Bridgehampton National Bank
The Nature Conservancy
Allan M. Schneider Associates, Inc.
Roberta Gosman Donovan
North Fork Bank
Group for the South Fork, Inc.
Shinnecock Fish Dock, Inc.
The Suffolk County National Bank
The Bank of the Hamptons, N.A.
Ivy Acres, Inc.
Shinnecock Fisherman's Cooperative Association, Inc.
Long Island Farm Bureau
Oakland Marina
Riverhead Townscape, Inc.
Long Island Seafood Export, Inc.
Bedell Vineyards, Inc.
North Fork Environmental Council, Inc.
Gristina Vineyards
Long Island Inshore Trawlermen's Association, Inc.
Stephen J. Patterson, III
Edwin Fishel Tuccio
Coecles Harbor Marina & Boatyard, Inc.
Montauk Boatmen and Captains Association, Inc.
Captain's Cove Marina

Governor's Appointments to the End End Economic Task Force
Five East End Town Supervisors and Mayors' Representative as *ex officio* members

Fred Thiele
Southampton

Scott Harris
Southold

Joseph Janoski
Riverhead

Huson Sherman
Shelter Island

Tony Bullock
East Hampton

Paul Rickenbach, Mayor
Village of East Hampton

Tom Twomey, Chair

Agricultural Industry
Joseph Gergela, Work Group Chair, Long Island Farm Bureau

Brenda Filmanski, Planner
Town of Riverhead

Ed Merz, President
Suffolk Co. Nat. Bank

Bill Sanok, Director
Agricultural Research
Cornell Cooperative
Extension

Cliff Foster
Farmer, Bridgehampton

Jack Van de Wetering
Farmer, Calverton

Robert Hartmann
Retired Farmer, Riverhead

Curtis Highsmith
Riverhead Chamber of Commerce

Lyle Wells, President
Long Island Farm Bureau

Ray Wesnofske
Retired Farmer

Recreational/Second Home Industry
Kevin McDonald, Work Group Chair, Group for the South Fork

Thomas Tobin, President
Bridgehampton Nat. Bank

Nancy Nagle Kelley
Associate Director of Development and
Government Relations
Guild Hall of East Hampton

Sharon Kast, Chair
Mashomack Presever
Nature Conservancy
Shelter Island

Peter Hallock, President
Allan M. Schneider & Associates

Chris Hogan
Community Leader

Steve Kenny
Professor of Economics
Suffolk County Community College,
Riverhead

Tom Whelan
Riverhead Attorney

Helen Hillman
Mrs. Condie Lamb Agency

Roberta Gosman Donovan
Restauranteur, Montauk

Peter Needham
Marina Operator

Sherry Patterson
Real Estate Broker, Riverhead;
Past Member, Riverhead Town Zoning
Board of Appeals

Bran Ferren, President
Associates & Ferren

John Scheetz, South Fork
Promotion Committee

Betty Brown, Former Pres.,
North Fork Environmental Council;
Vice-Pres., Save the
Bays, Riverhead

Sara Davison, Director
The Nature Conservancy

Fishing Industry
Larry Cantwell, Work Group Chair; Commissioner, Atlantic State Marine Fisheries Commission

Lisa Liquori, Planner
Town of East Hampton

Kathy Francis, Sr. Vice-Pres.
Bank of the Hamptons

Rowland F. Clark
Commercial Fisherman

Risk Lofstad, Director
Fishermen's Co-op

John Scotti, Director
Sea Grant Program
Cornell Cooperative Extension

Marybess Phillips, Owner
Commercial Fishing Vessel

Joe McBride, President
Montauk Captains' Assn.

Wine Industry
Carol Gristina, Work Group Chair, Gristina Vineyards

Robert Kassner, Site Plan
Reviewer, Town of Southold

John Kanas, President
North Fork Bank & Trust Co.

Louisa Hargrave, Vintner
Hargrave Vineyards

Alice Wise, Viticulturist
Cornell Cooperative Extension

Robert Palmer, Owner &
Winemaker, Palmer Vineyards

Kep Bedell, Owner &
Winemaker, Bedell Vineyards

BLUEPRINT FOR OUR FUTURE

BLUEPRINT FOR OUR FUTURE

Creating Jobs, Preserving the Environment

The Report to Governor Mario Cuomo

BY THE EAST END ECONOMIC & ENVIRONMENTAL TASK FORCE OF LONG ISLAND, NEW YORK

Tom Twomey, Chairman

Joseph Gergela, Agriculture   Carol Gristina, Wine Industry
Larry Cantwell, Fishing   Kevin McDonald, Recreation
Nancy Nagle Kelley, Editor

Newmarket Press   New York

Copyright © 1994 The East End Economic and Environmental
Institute, Inc.

This book published simultaneously in the
United States of America and in Canada

All rights reserved. This book may not be reproduced, in whole or in part, in any form, without written permission. Inquiries should be addressed to Permissions Department, Newmarket Press, 18 East 48th Street, New York, NY 10017

94 95 96 97   10 9 8 7 6 5 4 3 2 1

Library of Congress Cataloging-in-Publication Data
East End Economic & Environmental Task Force of Long Island, New York
Blueprint for our future: creating jobs, preserving the environment/The East End Economic & Environmental Task Force of Long Island, New York.
p.   cm.
ISBN 1-55704-202-0
1. East End (Long Island, N.Y.)-Economic policy.
2. Environmental policy-New York (State)-East End (Long Island)
I. Title
HC107.N72E184   1994
338.9747'21-dc20
93-51076
CIP

Quantity purchases
Companies, professional groups, clubs and other organizations may qualify for special terms when ordering quantities of this title. For information, write Special Sales Department, Newmarket Press, 18 East 48th Street, New York, NY 10017, or call (212) 832-3575

Manufactured in the United States of America

First Edition

Table of Contents

Foreword	*Governor Mario Cuomo*	Page xiii
Map of East End		xiv
Introduction	Tom Twomey, Chair	1

Recommendations

AGRICULTURAL INDUSTRY

	INDUSTRY OVERVIEW *by Joe Gergela,* *Executive Secretary, Long Island Farm Bureau*	9
1	A New York Farmland Preservation Program Should Be Created	11
2	An East End Agricology Institute Should Be Created	15
3	Funds for Applied Agricultural Research and Education Should Be Increased	20
4	More Agricultural Parcels Should Be Eligible for Agricultural Assessment	24
5	Horse Boarding Operations Should Be Eligible for Agricultural Assessment	26
6	A "Grown on Long Island" Campaign Should Be Promoted	27

FISHING INDUSTRY

INDUSTRY OVERVIEW *by Larry Cantwell, Commissioner, Atlantic State Marine Fisheries Commission*   *31*

7   A Program of Stormwater Run-Off Remediation, Land Use Control, and Strategic Land Acquisitions Should Be Carried Out by Local, County and State Governments in the Peconic Bay Estuary Area   *33*

8   An Oyster Mariculture Training Program for Eastern Long Island Commercial Fishermen Should Be Created   *35*

9   A Funding Program to Finance Fish Processing Facilities Should Be Developed   *38*

10   Sales Tax Exemption of Fuel Purchases at the Pump for Commercial Fishermen Should Be Adopted   *42*

11   Unemployment Insurance Benefits for Fishing Crew Members Should Not Be Required   *44*

12   Shinnecock Commercial Dock Facilities Should Be Expanded   *46*

13   East End Shellfish Resources Located in Uncertified Shellfishing Areas Should Be Managed Through Control Purification (Depuration)   *48*

14   A Fisheries Management Process Should Be Formally Created Within DEC   *51*

15   The Shinnecock Inlet Erosion Project Should Be Completed On an Emergency Basis   *53*

16   Aquaculture Should Be Supported   *54*

17   New York Seafood Council Marketing and Promotional Efforts Should Be Supported by a Permanent Funding Mechanism   *57*

Contents ix

WINERY INDUSTRY

INDUSTRY OVERVIEW *by Carol Gristina, Gristina Vineyards & Alice Wise, Viticulturist, Cornell Cooperative Extension*   61

18   A Viticulture Conference Should Be Held on the East End   66

19   Funding for Vinifera Wine and Grape Research Should Be Increased   74

20   Long Island Wines Should Be Promoted   81

21   The Grape Price Law Should Exempt Vinifera Grapes   83

RECREATION/SECOND HOME INDUSTRY

INDUSTRY OVERVIEW *by Kevin McDonald, Group for the South Fork & Nancy Nagle Kelley, Guild Hall*   87

Natural Resources

22   The Land Acquisition Partnership Between the State and Local Governments Should Be Expanded   91

23   Existing Regulatory Environmental Objectives Should Be Supplemented with Incentives   95

24   Enforcement of Tidal and Freshwater Wetland Laws Should Be Delegated to Towns and Villages   100

Transportation

OVERVIEW   103

25   A Park and Rail for Residents and Visitors to the East End and Other Transportation Improvements Should Be Constructed   105

26   A Shuttle Rail Service to Run Between Villages Should Be Implemented   108

27   A Network of Bike Paths Should Be Created   109

Contents

Marinas

OVERVIEW *by Peter Needham, Marine Operator*   *111*

28   Programs to Retain Marina Facilities on the East End Should Be Created   *114*

29   Financial and Technical Assistance for Marina and Boatyard Environmental Infrastructure Improvements Should Be Provided   *117*

30   The Permit System for Marinas Should Be Streamlined and Simplified   *119*

31   Recent Amendments to the Navigation Law Should Be Revised to Assure Equitable Access to Coastal Waters for All New York Residents   *121*

Tourism

32   A Tourist Plan for the East End Should Be Jointly Funded by the State and Local Governments   *122*

33   The "I Love NY" Campaign Should Promote the East End   *125*

34   The 5% Luxury Tax on Hotels Should Be Repealed   *127*

35   The Jobs Development Authority Should Be Authorized to Enable Tourism Facilities to Benefit   *128*

36   A Marketing Survey to Identify Potential Markets and Visitors' Needs and Maximize Benefits Derived from Tourism Advertising Dollars Should Be Jointly Funded   *130*

37   Tourist Information Centers Should Be Established   *131*

REGIONAL ISSUES

38   The Creation of an East End Education Center at the Eastern Campus of Suffolk Community College Should Be Further Studied   *135*

		Contents	
39		Fairness and Flexibility for University Medical Center at Stony Brook Should Be Enacted	140
40		Worker's Compensation Reform Should Be Adopted	142
41		Reasonable Return on Property Should Be Recognized in State Legislation	145
42		Mandate Relief Should Be Adopted	146
43		The Proposed Jetport at Calverton Should Be Opposed	149
44		Matching State Funding for Study of Financial Feasibility of Forming Peconic County Should Be Supported	150
		Biographies of Governor's Appointees	153

See Page

APPENDICES

Agriculture

A	24	Draft Bill S 4654 to amend the Agriculture & Markets Law in relation to agricultural assessments	173
B	26	Draft Bill A 4806 to amend the Agriculture & Markets Law in relation to the definition of land use in agricultural production	174

Fishing

C	31	Fisheries Landing Statistics for States of New York, New Jersey, Connecticut, and Rhode Island	175
D	31	The First Annual Report on the Status of U.S. Living Marine Resources	176
E	33	Brown Tide Comprehensive Assessment and Management Program Summary prepared by the Suffolk County Department of Health Services, dated November, 1992	178

F	34	*Newsday* article entitled "Voters Asked to Finance Bay Cleanup," dated July 14, 1993	180
G	38	*Newsday* article entitled "Casting a Wider Net," dated June 14, 1993	181
H	40	Report of Sales of fish products from the Office of General Services, Division of Supply Support, to the various State facilities for fiscal year ending March 31, 1993	183
I	52	Draft Bill Memo dated 12/30/92 introduced by N.Y.S. Assemblyman Thomas P. DiNapoli to amend Environmental Conservation Law in relation to marine fisheries to enhance the State's management program	185
J	52	East Hampton Town Baymen's Association proposal for legislation dated August 11, 1993	188

Recreation/Second Home Industry

K	91	Community Appearance and Tourism: What's the Link? by Edward T. McMahon	192
L	92	"The Economic Benefits of Land Conservation" by Holly L. Thomas, Senior Planner, Dutchess County Planning Department	194
M	123	*Newsday* "Viewpoints" article entitled "Goodwill Games Should Swim East," dated 11/12/92	198
N	125	1993 Budget for "I Love NY" Program	199
O	124	Detailed Plan for the Preservation of the East End Maritime Heritage & Restoration of Greenport's Deep-Water Harbor Facilities	200
P	124	Proposed Budget for Railroad Museum of Long Island	203
Q	91	State Ownership of Land in the Five East End Towns	204

Foreword

NEARLY ONE YEAR AGO, in response to a sensible request by local business, government and community leaders, I created the first Economic and Environmental Task Force for the East End of Long Island in New York State's history.

The Task Force grew from the recognition by the leadership of Long Island's East End of the need to plot a future course for their five towns—Riverhead, Southampton, East Hampton, Shelter Island and Southold—that accommodated both environmental and economic concerns.

The 49 Task Force members—public officials, bank presidents, farmers, environmentalists, commercial fishermen, motel and marina operators, vineyard and restaurant owners, and real estate brokers—worked diligently throughout 1993, donating substantial time to the people of New York State.

Working without a budget and without a staff, this dedicated and talented group of New Yorkers focused on four key areas of importance to the unique East End of Long Island:

1) the Agricultural Industry;
2) the Fishing Industry;
3) the Winery Industry;
4) the Recreation/Second Home Industry.

Task Force members did their work with a high degree of vigor and intensity, collectively contributing hundreds of hours of work and agreeing upon a wide-ranging set of 44 recommendations.

Their effort was bipartisan, and they kept small differences over the shadings of issues from clouding their effort to present a coherent picture of how life could be better on the magnificent East End of Long Island.

The Task Force members deserve our gratitude for their selfless commitment to the well-being of their fellow Long Islanders, and our admiration for a vision as clear as the sun rising out of the sparkling Atlantic waters off the Island's East End.

Governor Mario Cuomo

Albany, New York　　　　　　　　　　　　　　　　　　　　*December, 1993*

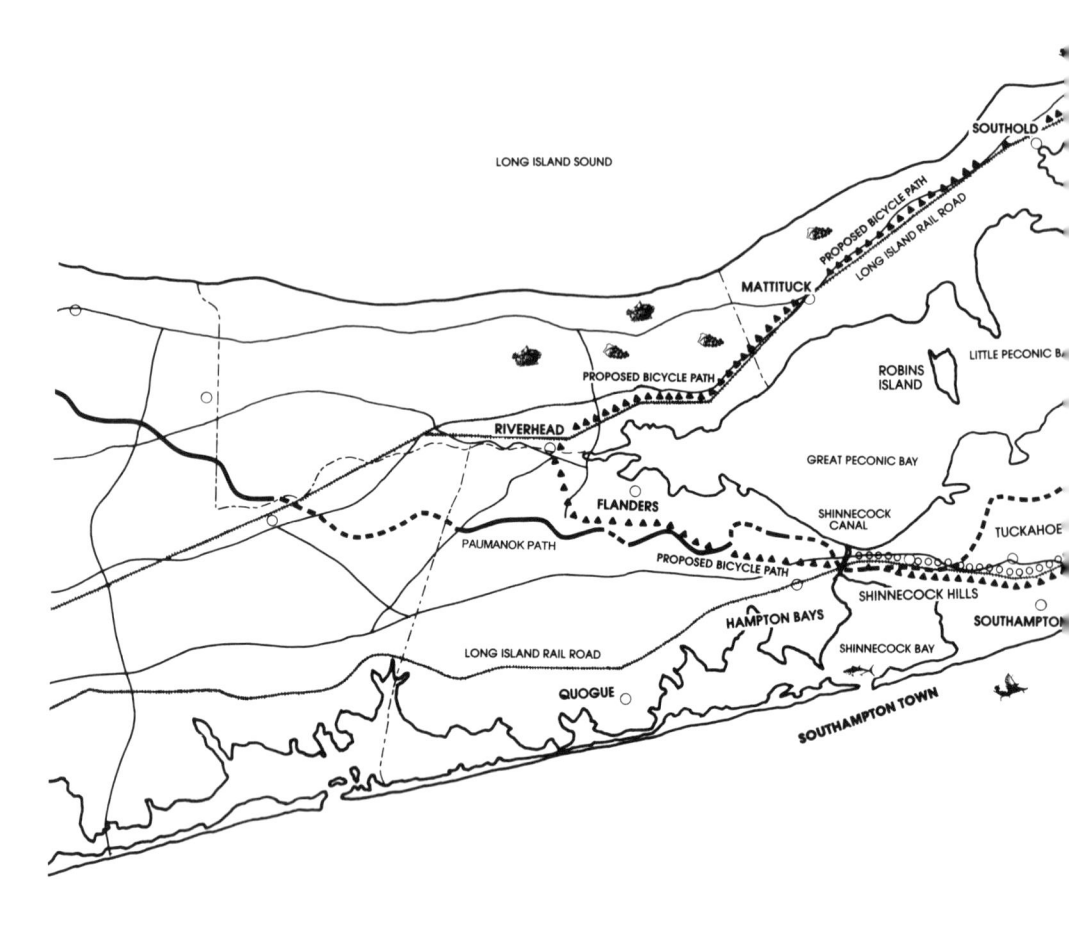

GOVERNOR CUOMO'S EAST END ENVIRONMENTAL AND ECONOMIC TASK FORCE

Tom Twomey, Chair

AGRICULTURAL INDUSTRY

Joseph Gergela, Chair
Long Island Farm Bureau

Map of Eastern Long Island

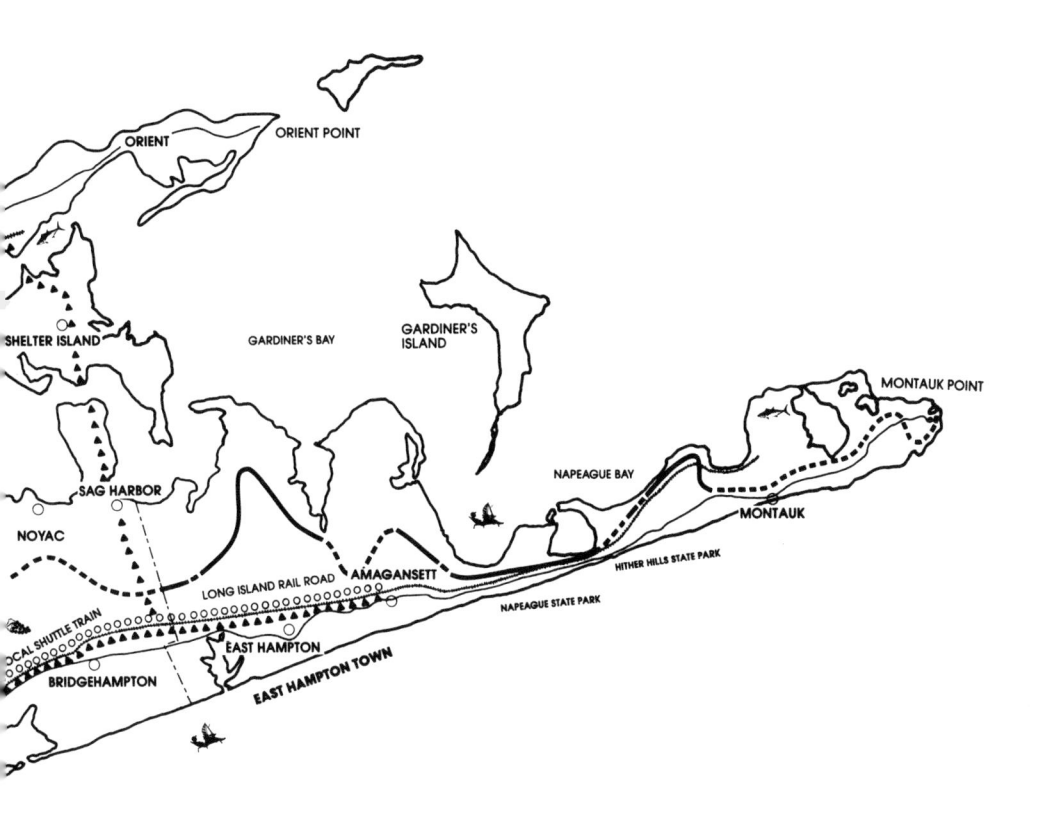

Locations: ORIENT, ORIENT POINT, SHELTER ISLAND, GARDINER'S BAY, GARDINER'S ISLAND, MONTAUK POINT, NAPEAGUE BAY, MONTAUK, SAG HARBOR, NOYAC, LONG ISLAND RAIL ROAD, AMAGANSETT, HITHER HILLS STATE PARK, NAPEAGUE STATE PARK, LOCAL SHUTTLE TRAIN, EAST HAMPTON, BRIDGEHAMPTON, EAST HAMPTON TOWN

LEGEND
- ━ ━ ━ PAUMANOK PATH
- ooooooooooo PROPOSED LOCAL SHUTTLE TRAIN
- ▬▬▬▬▬ LONG ISLAND RAILROAD
- ▲▲▲▲▲▲▲▲ PROPOSED BICYCLE PATH

SCALE IN MILES
0 1 2 3 4 5

RECREATIONAL/2ND HOME INDUSTRY
Kevin McDonald, Chair
Group for the South Fork

FISHING INDUSTRY
Larry Cantwell, Chair
Atlantic State Marine Fisheries

WINE INDUSTRY
Carol Gristina, Chair
Gristina Vineyards

TOWN SUPERVISORS:
Tony Bullock, East Hampton
Joseph Janoski, Riverhead
Scott Harris, Southold
Huson Sherman, Shelter Island
Fred Thiele, Southampton

VILLAGE MAYORS:
Paul Rickenbach, East Hampton Village

BLUEPRINT FOR OUR FUTURE

Introduction

On January 13, 1993, Governor Mario Cuomo created history. On that date, the Governor established the East End Economic and Environmental Task Force.

> "There has been substantial debate over what is best for the future of this unique region of New York. This task force will rely on the information gathered from East End citizens to help plan for a secure future. Long Island's East End—comprised of the Towns of Riverhead, Southampton, East Hampton, Shelter Island and Southold—relies economically on agriculture, fishing, recreational industries and second home residents. Median family income on the East End is 20 percent less than comparable income for the rest of Nassau and Suffolk counties, largely because of the area's rural character."
>
> *Governor Mario Cuomo*

The Governor's appointments consisted of forty-nine individuals who reside on the East End: bank presidents, farmers, environmentalists, fishermen, motel and marine operators, vineyard and restaurant owners, and real estate brokers. Also included were members of the East End academic community including senior staff personnel from the Cornell Cooperative Extension located in Riverhead. Never before had a Governor of New York State convened such a Task Force of East End leaders to propose improvements to New York State law.

History was also made by the fact that it was the first time in recent memory that a New York Task Force was created with no staff, no executive director, no consultants, no money appropriated for any reason. The Governor directed this Task Force to report back to him before the end of the year with specific recommendations for inclusion in his 1994 State legislative package. The Governor realized that, with such a tight timetable, the individuals whom he appointed would have to do the work themselves, drawing on their own successful experiences, unfiltered by consultants and advisors. The Governor challenged these members of the community to join together in the spirit of public service for the benefit of the community.

Pivotal to the success of the Task Force was the Governor's appointment of the Supervisors of the five East End Towns and a representative of the eight Mayors from the area to participate in and review the work done by the Task Force. It is these public officials who constantly struggle to solve the problems of local residents. The Governor wanted their experience and valuable advice. The Supervisors, in turn, assigned professional planners from the Towns to assist the Task Force.

Purpose of the Task Force

THE GOVERNOR WAS very specific in his direction to the Task Force members. He wanted proposals which he could undertake, through legislation or executive action, to enhance the economy of the East End of Long Island without threatening its fragile environment. The Governor presented the group with seven specific questions and made it clear that he needed the recommendations of the Task Force by November, 1993 in order to include as many as possible into his 1994 legislative package submitted to the State Legislature with his State-of-the-State message in January of that year. In addition to specific legislative proposals, the Governor asked for other agency actions which he should implement. The Governor also asked the Task Force to include in these recommendations support he should give to improvements to statutes and regulations at the federal and local levels which did not specifically require state legislation.

Why Was a Task Force Needed?

FOR CENTURIES, the East End of Long Island has been secluded and remote from the rest of the economy of New York State. In fact, for several centuries, the East End was historically, culturally and economically more closely tied to Connecticut, Rhode Island, and the rest of New England than the State of New York. The original settlers of the five East End Towns came from Puritan communities dotting the shores of Massachusetts and Connecticut, rather than from the rest of Long Island, much less New York City. When the towns were originally settled approximately 350 years ago, the predominant mode of transportation was by ship. As a result, the East End's economic ties were with New England, which was much closer and easier to communicate with than New York City.

The railroad was constructed 200 years after the East End Towns were founded. Prior to the railroad, there were only a few rutted dirt roads connecting the East End to New York.

Introduction

As a result of several centuries of relative isolation, the culture and economy of the East End evolved differently from the rest of Long Island. Even today, few residents of the area commute to the City of New York for employment. Most of the residents of the East End have chosen to come or stay here knowing full well they will earn less than if they moved further west. Yet, they have chosen the East End as their home due to its rural lifestyle and environment.

Farming, fishing, and vineyards are the most visible industry of the area. In fact, Suffolk County is the number one agricultural county in New York State. However, there is probably no other area in New York State which has benefited from such a huge investment of capital invested by individuals primarily for recreational purposes. The owners of these second homes are usually individuals who live much of the year elsewhere, predominantly in the City of New York. Due to the rural quality of the East End, they have chosen to collectively invest approxmately $10 billion in the community which, in turn, produces a substantial multiplier effect in the local economy. At the outset, real estate brokers and construction and renovation contractors receive the benefit of this investment. For years thereafter, the second homeowner continues to spend large sums in the community in addition to local real estate taxes. Not just during the summer, but on numerous weekends throughout the year, second homeowners spend thousands of dollars in local hardware stores, clothing stores, book stores, and throughout the rest of Main Street. Restaurant owners, marina operators and other recreation businesses receive annually the benefit from this $10 billion investment, as do homeowner service industries, such as plumbers, electricians, landscape nurseries, and home insurance brokers.

However, like any other investment, this one could turn sour if the reason the second homeowners have invested so much on the East End disappears. If the beaches of the East End become polluted, or if agriculture and fishing vanished, these second homeowners would have no reason to maintain their investment on the East End. They would choose to relocate to a less spoiled second-home area. If that should occur, the East End economy would crash.

How the Task Force Was Organized

RECOGNIZING THIS FACT, the Task Force set about its work by dividing itself into four work groups. The first two concentrated on the agriculture and fishing industries—historically, the predominant cash crops of the area. These two industries are threatened by market forces and regulatory action which could render them non-competitive nationwide. If such occurs, these industries will become extinct on the East End. In addition to the economic turmoil this would create in terms of loss revenue and jobs, the demise of these industries would seriously undercut the viability of the $10 billion investment made by the second homeowner. Each of these work groups have developed recommendations which would reverse the projected decline in jobs and revenue forecasted for these industries. The recommendations would rejuvenate and revitalize both economic sectors for generations to come.

The third work group analyzed the relatively new wine industry on the East End. This industry offers great promise for importing dollars to the East End economy while, at the same time, providing further underpinnings for the second home industry. In recent years, 17 wineries have opened on the East End producing world-class, award-winning vintages. Unlike any other wine produced in New York State, the East End wines are rated higher than many French and Californian wines. The combination of near-perfect soil and optimal number of days of sun have produced wines of great quality. This work group has made recommendations to significantly expand this industry on the East End through a relatively minimum investment by the State of New York.

The last work group focused on the recreational industry. This work group analyzed why the second homeowners have collectively invested billions in the area, what it would take to nurture this investment and to prevent it from leaving the area which, as stated earlier, would create severe economic decline. Since most on the Task Force agree that the prime motivation for this investment is recreational, this work group concentrated on enhancements to the recreation opportunities afforded the residents of the East End, including second homeowners, as well as the recreational opportunities offered to non-residents of the area. The recommendations of this work group concentrate on further land acquisition necessary to maintain the rural character of the area, additional investments in beaches, marinas, bike paths, and transportation to service this industry.

Each of the Task Force's work groups has made recommendations to modify certain regulatory rules and regulations which unwittingly undermine the viability of the East End economy. Where appropriate, the work groups have recommended new legislation or technical fixes to existing legislation to implement their proposals. In other instances, specific changes to a section of the Code of Rules and Regulations promulgated by the Executive Branch have been proposed.

Altogether, there are 44 recommendations being made in this report. Noticeably absent are recommendations that deal with statewide issues which are not germane to, or arise from, the East End. The Task Force felt it would better serve the residents of the East End if it dealt only with those issues that were uniquely East End issues.

Introduction

In addition to serving as a set of specific proposals for the Governor and the State Legislature to consider in the 1994 legislative session, we hope that this report will serve as a guide to others in the East End community who wish to become involved in affecting its future. To the extent that not every recommendation in this report is immediately adopted by the State Legislature, this document can serve as a blueprint or an agenda for future decision-making regarding the East End.

In addition to the seven plenary sessions of the Task Force to produce this report, the work groups met dozens of times as part of the process. This report, which is the result of this collective effort, represents the thousands of hours of public service donated by some of the most dedicated individuals on the East End.

Each member of the Task Force must be thanked and congratulated for this effort. In particular, those who served as Chairs of work groups need to be given special recognition for the enormous effort they made on behalf of the community. Larry Cantwell, Joe Gergela, Carol Gristina and Kevin McDonald each deserve this special thanks. Bill Sanok, John Scotti, and Alice Wise from Cornell Cooperative Extension provided a great deal of technical assistance without which this report would not have been possible. In addition, Nancy Nagle Kelley, who edited the report, and Janice Olsen, who typed and produced it, both need to be recognized for the many hours spent on this effort. We also thank Supervisors Hoot Sherman, Fred Thiele, Tony Bullock, Joe Janoski and Scott Harris and Mayor Paul Rickenbach who made substantial contributions to all of the recommendations contained in this report. Also, Congressman George Hochbrueckner and New York State Senator Kenneth LaValle are owed a debt of gratitude for the assistance they and their staffs rendered in the preparation of this report. A special thanks must also be given to members of the Governor's staff who provided valuable support for this Task Force: Andrew Zambelli, Secretary to the Governor; Ellen Conovitz, Director of Administration; Steve Villano, former Director of the New York City Press Office; and Mark Grossman, the Governor's Long Island Regional Representative.

Lastly, we thank Governor Mario Cuomo for creating this Task Force and for listening to the people of the East End.

In Conclusion

THE WORK OF the Task Force has brought together much of the government, business, agricultural and environmental leadership of the East End with one goal in mind: to strengthen the East End economy without adversely affecting its environment. Committed to the East End's long-term growth, sharing the same goals, the Task Force members arduously worked and compromised until 44 recommendations were unanimously agreed upon.

The first theme which runs throughout the report is the need for simple fairness for the people of the East End. The report calls for a level playing field for the East End so it can effectively compete to survive as a vital economic resource for the State. Several recommendations call for additional funding. Often, this is matched by an offer by the East End Towns for joint funding of a particular proposal. Other times, the request is made to rectify a detrimental imbalance in prior funding formula which unfairly undercuts the East End's efforts to help itself.

The second theme running throughout the recommendations is the call for positive, enlightened governmental action to help better train and better educate the East End work force. The East End Agricology Institute described in this report, if developed to its full potential, will do just that.

As Governor Cuomo has said, "We need to have government help improve education, offer more job training and improve production methods as well as research and development. It takes more than speeches; it takes revenues."

This Task Force is acutely aware that State revenues are in short supply. However, we believe our recommendations are fair and reasonable. We believe that the East End is a valuable resource for all of the people of New York State—an area which deserves the benefit of some hard and smart decisions by the Governor and the State Legislature to give us the wherewithal to do the things we need to do.

Tom Twomey
November, 1993

AGRICULTURAL INDUSTRY

Overview

AGRICULTURAL INDUSTRY

JOE GERGELA
Executive Secretary, Long Island Farm Bureau

AGRICULTURE HAS LONG been a mainstay of the East End of Long Island. The sandy loam soils, deposited over 10,000 years ago by glacial action, are well-drained and productive. Three surrounding bodies of water—Peconic Bay, Long Island Sound and the Atlantic Ocean—moderate the climate, providing a long-growing season, warm, sunny summers and falls, and a mild winter. For these reasons, agriculture on Long Island is diverse, ranging from traditional potato and vegetable fields to greenhouses, nursery stock, fruit trees, and vineyards.

Agriculture continues to be an important industry in Suffolk County as it provides fresh food, fiber and horticultural products for our residents, preserves wildlife habitat and esthetic beauty and contributes to our quality of life.

Perhaps, even more important, farmland provides a buffer against urban sprawl and maintains the traditional rural character of Eastern Suffolk. Agriculture is important to the tourism industry as it provides the landscape and destination tourists seek. Tourism is now Long Island's largest industry with over $1 billion each year attributed to this industry. It is estimated that over 25 million persons visit the East End annually. Agriculture helps provide the scenic vistas desired by our visitors. It also provides proximity to farm markets where visitors and year-round residents enjoy the advantage of locally produced fruits, vegetables, ornamental horticultural products and wine. The East End's emerging wine industry provides over $2 million annually to the state coffers in sales tax revenue. In addition, wineries increase the attractiveness of the East End as a tourist destination.

Agriculture is a significant economic contributor in Suffolk County to the tune of over $150,000,000 in annual sales of agricultural products, making the County the leading agricultural county in the Empire State and among the top ten in the United States. There is agreement among residents and leaders of Suffolk County that the agricultural industry is crucial to our economic well-being. Saving farmland and maintaining a viable agricultural industry makes economic sense for the county. The conversion of farmland to development creates an additional property tax burden and increases demand for government services. According to a recent study conducted by the American Farmland Trust, farming requires a cost of services of 21¢ for every dollar paid in local property taxes. This compares to 29¢ for commercial properties and $1.36 for residential property.

Agriculture on Long Island centers upon high-return crops, such as flowers, nursery stock, fruit, grapes, and vegetables. Direct marketing of produce through garden centers, wineries, and farmstands has become the standard. With an increasing population in farming areas and concern over groundwater quality, the methods of farming must be environmentally sensitive methods. Agricultural research and education is the only legitimate means of generating the information required by today's farmers. Many branches of Cornell University have provided invaluable assistance to local industries, including the Long Island Horticultural Research Lab, Cornell Cooperative Extension of Suffolk County, the New York State Agricultural Experiment Station, and other departments in Cornell's College of Ag and Life Sciences. Continued support and funding of the state's agricultural researchers will provide environmentally sensitive production methods which ensure economic viability.

As farmers continue to operate on Eastern Long Island, major efforts have been made to preserve both the quality of our open space resources and the underlying aquifer. The Integrated Pest Management Program ("IPM") from Cornell Cooperative Extension encourages growers to use the latest and most environmentally safe practices in controlling insects, diseases and weeds. Thresholds, biological and cultural practices and more efficient pesticide use have resulted in a decreased potential for groundwater contamination, as well as savings to producers. As the dynamics of agriculture continue, the trend is toward a higher return and higher capital investment requiring less land and a more intensive, well-trained labor force.

The following pages describe actions we recommend the Governor take in order to insure the continued viability and growth of agriculture on the East End.

Recommendation #1:

A NEW YORK STATE FARMLAND PRESERVATION PROGRAM SHOULD BE CREATED

Background

SUFFOLK COUNTY WAS ONE of the first regions in the country to recognize that preservation of agricultural land would not be possible without a public program. Therefore, in 1974, Suffolk County instituted the first Purchase of Development Rights Program (PDR) in the country. This program is still active today with over 7,000 acres preserved in perpetuity in both Suffolk County and town PDR programs. In such a program, the landowner retains the title and all associated ownership rights except for the right to build on or develop the property. In return, the landowner receives a payment equal to the value of development rights.

While substantial amounts of farmland have been protected through these programs, it is estimated that an additional 10,000 acres of farmland on the East End must be preserved in order to sustain a viable agricultural industry.

The Suffolk County Farmland Preservation Program

IN 1973, a fourteen-member Agricultural Advisory Committee was appointed by then-County Executive, John V.N. Klein. In the same year, the Suffolk County Planning Commission, under the direction of Lee Koppelman, prepared a Farmland Preservation Program report to the County Legislature. That report stressed the importance of agriculture while noting changing land use patterns and the pressure leading to conversion of farmland to residential development.

The Agricultural Advisory Committee to County Executive Klein found that of the approximately 68,000 acres in farmland in Suffolk County in 1973, 30,000 acres should be protected through the acquisition of development rights. In order to protect agriculture, the industry, as well as the land, must be preserved. A critical mass of agricultural activities must exist for agriculture to continue.

Although the success of the Suffolk County Purchase of Development Rights Program has served as a model for other areas in the country and has been augmented by municipal Purchase of Development Rights Programs, the program has fallen short of its original goal of 30,000 acres of protected farmland.

In early 1974, the Agricultural Advisory Committee released a report to the legislature recommending an expenditure of 45-to-50-million dollars over the next three years to purchase the development rights on farmland. (Appraisers typically think of the development rights value of land as three-fourths of the total market value of land and the agricultural value as one-fourth of market value.)

Farmers embraced the program as a means to capitalize on equity during their lifetimes and, at the same time, devalue the property to ensure the land could be passed on to future generations by reducing the estate tax burden.

The Committee recommended proceeding with the program on the following basis:

1. Acquisition of development rights as opposed to acquisition of fee title. Use of the properties stripped of development values would be for agricultural purposes only and fee title retained by the farmer. The development values or rights would be held in perpetuity by Suffolk County. Under the New York State Real Property Tax Law, property taxes are based on full and best use; therefore, taxes would be assessed for the agricultural use of the property since that would be the highest and best use.

2. Farms to be preserved would be carefully chosen to constitute relatively large parcels and in areas where contiguous parcels could be preserved at a later date. Isolated farms would not be conducive to continued operation because of non-farm influence on them.

3. Preserved farms should be bounded by roads, highways, and open space to provide a buffer zone between farm activities and nearby residential or commercial uses.

4. Development rights, once purchased by the County, could not be sold without affirmative voter approval by referendum as is the case with preserves or trusts under the County Charter.

5. Program participation would be on a voluntary basis by members of the farm community without resort by the County.

In the summer of 1974, a Farmland Select Committee was established and began the solicitation process on a county-wide basis. The procedure allowed the Committee to make recommendations on parcels to be included in the program with final approval by the County Legislature. Local Law #19-1974 officially authorized the Agricultural Program, and $21 million was appropriated to purchase development rights under Phase I. In early 1975, the first bids were opened on Phase I of the program and sixty bids were received on 3,883 acres.

In September of 1976, the legislature allocated the $21 million authorized under Phase I. On September 29, 1977, the first farmland development rights were purchased on 131 acres in the Town of Riverhead and 84 acres in Aquebogue. Phase II of the PDR program began in July, 1978 when bids for 249 properties on some 11,356 acres were received.

In 1980, a new County Executive, Peter F. Cohalan, recommended an additional $10 million be authorized to continue funding the programs which would bring the total County commitment to $31 million. He also called for assistance from the towns in terms of large-lot zoning and cluster development to preserve additional farmland.

In 1988, County Executive Patrick Halpin recommended adding a third phase to the farmland program. The legislature authorized $5 million in 1989 and $5 million in 1990 for Phase III. The first 22 acres of Phase III were acquired in 1989.

Current County Executive, Robert Gaffney, has requested $1 million each year for 1993, 1994 and 1995 to continue purchases under Phase III. Current fiscal problems have decimated the County's ability to fund the program at previous levels. At this time, there are approximately 3,000 acres on the list to be acquired by Suffolk County. An additional 7,000 acres would be sought to complete the program.

In addition, East Hampton, Southampton and Southold Towns, which have substantial amounts of farmland, initiated local programs using town funds to purchase development rights to 121 acres, 711 acres and 252 acres, respectively, using the same criteria as Suffolk County.

New York State Farmland Preservation Program

A NEW YORK STATE Farmland Preservation Program should be created to fund a purchase of development rights program similar to the one pioneered by Suffolk County. The State program would be on a 50% matching fund basis, coordinated and administered by counties in the State, consistent with the goals set forth in the Agricultural Protection Act of 1992. That Act encourages a comprehensive farmland protection plan under 25AA of the New York Agriculture and Markets Law. The funding for this program would come from the provisions of the Environmental Protection Act signed into law in 1993. The program would be established statewide and implemented in any county which has established its own farmland protection program. Under such a program, the development rights on an additional 10,000 acres could be preserved through matching funds with the County and Town programs in existence in Suffolk County. *Once this additional farmland is preserved, the critical mass of productive farmland to sustain a viable agricultural industry on the East End will be guaranteed.*

Section 302 of the Agriculture and Markets Law would be expanded to empower the Farmland Protection Board currently created thereunder to certify to the Commissioner of Agriculture and Markets those parcels for joint funding by the County and State programs. The program would be strictly voluntarily on the part of the property owner.

In order for a parcel to be deemed eligible for funding by the state program, it must be (i) certified by the county agency administering the county program that the parcel meets the eligibility requirements for inclusion in the local program, making it thereby eligible for county payment of one-half the cost of acquisition of the development rights; and (ii) certified by the County Agriculture and Farmland Protection Board that it meets the county agriculture and farmland protection plan provided for in 302 of Article 25AA.

The program would provide that on June 1st of each year, or sooner, the Commissioner of Agriculture and Markets would review said certifications from each county board made during the prior twelve months and include the certified parcels on the Department's list of eligible parcels for the New York State Farmland Protection Program. The Commissioner would annually, or at other appropriate intervals, apply for funding under the provisions of the Environmental Protection Act. The Commissioner would develop criteria for the allocation of funds on an equitable basis throughout the State in the event in any given year there are insufficient state funds available to acquire all of the development rights for the certified parcels on a matching fund basis.

Proposed Action by the Governor:

THE GOVERNOR SHOULD introduce legislation amending Article 25AA of the Agriculture and Markets Law to provide for the establishment of a New York State Farmland Preservation Program which, in turn, could purchase the development rights from an additional 10,000 acres of farmland in Suffolk County and enable agriculture to remain a viable industry on the East End.

Recommendation #2:

AN EAST END AGRICOLOGY INSTITUTE SHOULD BE CREATED

Background

FOR SUFFOLK COUNTY to remain as the number one agricultural county in the State, the industry must adapt to changing environmental constraints and regulatory concerns. The harvesting of fish and shellfish are included in the broad definition of agriculture in New York State, as is the growing of grapes for wine production. The economic multiplier effect on the East End of the agriculture, fishing and wine industries is enormous. The direct impact of these agriculturally based industries on the tourism and second-home markets is well-established. The tourism and second-home industries, in turn, drive the construction, real estate and service industries of the area.

Therefore, the area's agricultural, fishing and wine industries are seminal and fundamental to the East End's economic health. Yet, the need for clean drinking water and clean bays and harbors is critical to the area remaining attractive to those who have invested $10 billion in the area for second homes. Few places in America provide such a clear example of the need for agricultural and environmental concerns to successfully co-exist. The East End is a relatively small land mass surrounded by bays and harbors. Its rural environment, so close to the New York Metropolitan region, has created high real estate values, adding pressure on the basic economy, which does not exist in other parts of the state.

Due to these factors, the need arises for an East End Agricology Institute to help solve the economic and environmental problems unique to the area. Such an Institute would engage in applied research and educational programs. It would develop improved methods for production for the agricultural, fishing and wine-growing industries so that they can economically prosper in the years ahead. Such prosperity would not only create significant numbers of new jobs in these particular industries, but would also guarantee a continuation of the second-home and recreation industries. The Institute would provide research support for these industries within the environmental constraints of the fragile ecology of the area. Further, research could directly benefit the environment if applied towards supporting emerging technologies which could help to preserve the ecology and the East End well into the next century. Such technologies include developing uses and markets for recyclable materials in addition to compost. These new uses and materials might directly affect the defined industries in agriculture, fishing and wine, but will certainly impact other sectors of the economy as well and help to maintain the quality of life that we enjoy. Thus, the name "agricology," coined by this report to signify the concerns of the proposed Institute.

Senator Kenneth P. LaValle issued in May of 1993 a report entitled "The Riverhead Agricultural and Environmental Technology International Incubator Program" which supports funding to initiate a formal feasibility study for a small business incubator to be located at Calverton Airport. The primary purposes of the proposed project are to provide a stimulus to the agricultural and marine economies of Eastern Long Island and to encourage the establishment of new commercial enterprises for agri-business, the marine industry and environmental technology. This proposal grew out of a similar concept developed in 1992 by the Town of Riverhead. Perhaps, this project could be developed in conjunction with, and as a module of, the East End Agricology Institute.

The Institute could be jointly funded by the East End Towns and various existing programs of New York State.

An example of the work the East End Agricology Institute would undertake is the research described below to find economically feasible methods to use composted municipal solid wastes for agricultural purposes. Other research the Institute could help fund and oversee would be the following:

1. Agricultural Research (p. 11)
2. Oyster Mariculture Training Program (p. 35)
3. The Shellfish Depuration Program (p. 48)
4. Aquaculture Program (p. 54)
5. Wine and Grape Research (p. 74)
6. Support for emerging technologies (described in this section)

The Cornell Cooperative Extension, located in Riverhead, might be the lead agency for the activities of the Agricology Institute.

This Institute, under the title of East End Agricology Institute, would operate under overall guidance of an executive committee made up of representatives from the following:

Five East End Town Supervisors
Suffolk Community College at Riverhead
SUNY at Stony Brook
Cornell Cooperative Extension
New York State Health Department
New York State Department of Environmental Conservation
New York State Department of Agriculture & Markets
New York State Legislative Solid Waste Commission

Suffolk County Department of Health Services
Suffolk County Executive's Office
Suffolk County Planning

An Agricology Institute Advisory Committee would be created to set overall policy, give guidance to the working group, approve work plan, and evaluate the program and identify funds and resources. Membership would come from representatives of:

Five East End Towns
Suffolk Community College at Riverhead
Cornell Cooperative Extension
SUNY Stony Brook Waste Management Institute
Cornell Waste Management Institute
Brookhaven National Laboratory
Suffolk County Department of Health Services
Suffolk County Planning
Compost Facility Manager
Long Island Farm Bureau
Long Island Farmer
Suffolk County Soil and Water Conservation District
Environmental Interest Group
Compost Facility Manager
Consumer

Composting

A SPECIFIC EXAMPLE OF the type of practical work to be done by the Institute is in the area of composting.

Organic products such as grass clippings, municipal yard waste, municipal solid waste and sewerage sludge have traditionally been landfilled in Suffolk County. Local municipalities are in desperate need of reducing the amount of waste materials through recycling and composting and are looking for markets and/or uses for these products. There is a developing interest in the use of the open space associated with agriculture to serve as a receiving point for these organic products, particularly, if they are composted.

The use of composted wastes on agricultural land has raised a number of questions concerning real and perceived hazards as well as the environmental and economic benefits. There is a need to control the source of raw materials to avoid contamination by heavy metals, organic chemicals, pathological organisms, and nonbiodegradable materials such as plastic and glass.

Some of these questions are already under investigation by cooperative projects:

1. A study of the use of composted municipal solid waste on a commercial sod planting with staff from the Waste Management Institute at Stony Brook, Cornell Cooperative Extension of Suffolk County, a local grower, and a private company.
2. The application of grass clippings on commercial vegetable farms, a cooperative effort between Cornell Cooperative Extension, local sweet corn growers, landscapers and towns on western Long Island.
3. There is a request for proposals to demonstrate the use of several compost materials on federal-aided highways in eastern Suffolk County.
4. Cornell Cooperative Extension has a project to conduct educational programs for county residents and to demonstrate recycling at the County Farm in Yaphank.

The agriculture committee has tried to address these issues from the perspective of the commercial farmer and land user.

In regard to the use of composted waste materials on open space, including farmland, a number of questions should be addressed by having applied research done by a combined effort with the New York State University at Stony Brook, Cornell University, Cornell Cooperative Extension, and possibly Brookhaven National Laboratory. As information and educational programs are developed, the potential to assist private enterprises in starting new businesses in the composting and application of raw and composted materials to open land is greatly increased.

It is essential that the coordinator of the Working Group be able to work with the towns, solid waste managers, private industry involved in composting, technical services and compost users to help facilitate the proper use of recycled organic materials. The Institute could be funded through New York State County Law 224B (Assembly Bill #8679, signed by the Governor on July 17, 1989, Chapter 575, Laws of 1989). Cornell Cooperative Extension of Suffolk County would be the recipient of these funds in support of a Long Island area program. With the Institute Coordinator stationed at the Cornell University Research Laboratory, applied research would be conducted on commercial farms in close cooperation with the East End towns but with information and educational programs applicable to all towns in Nassau and Suffolk Counties.

It is envisioned that the project coordinator would coordinate support for the applied research and educational programs through local municipalities and private composting businesses. Grants for specific projects would provide operating funds for the Institute. The towns could allocate their share of the funds from savings in disposal costs which are now spent in trucking and tipping fees at off-Long Island sites.

Cost of Establishing the East End Agricology Institute

	224B Funds	Matching
Personnel		
Institute Director or Coordinator	$ 60,000	
Personnel benefits, Office, travel	60,000	$ 60,000
Technician		30,000
Support Staff		30,000
Total	**$120,000**	**$120,000**

Proposed Action by the Governor:

THE GOVERNOR SHOULD support the creation of the East End Agricology Institute and direct his Commissioners of Agriculture and Markets, Environment, and Education to take the necessary steps to implement such a proposal in consultation with SUNY, the Cornell Cooperative Extension and other involved agencies and municipalities, including the five East End Towns.

Recommendation #3:

FUNDS FOR APPLIED AGRICULTURAL RESEARCH AND EDUCATION SHOULD BE INCREASED

Background

THERE ARE A NUMBER of characteristics that have placed Long Island in the forefront of economic and environmental concerns:

1. Agriculture continues to evolve as an intensive industry, dependent on a high-return cropping system such as that supplied by fruits, vegetables, nursery, grapes, flowers and direct-marketed crops. This, in turn, requires a reliance on the intense use of all phases of management and crop protection.

2. The large and increasing population of both Nassau and Suffolk Counties has exerted intense pressure on the use of open space, including agricultural lands, and other natural resources.

3. Long Island has been designated by the federal government as a sole source aquifer where groundwater is subject to contamination from the use of agricultural pesticides and fertilizers by farmers and homeowners due to Long Island's well-drained sandy soils.

4. Major strides have been made in reducing the use of agricultural chemicals by commercial producers and residents through such programs as Integrated Pest Management (IPM), the use of crop rotations, resistant varieties, beneficial predators, bio-pesticides, and other research-based educational programs.

5. Cornell Cooperative Extension of Suffolk County and the Long Island Horticultural Research Laboratory have played an important role in working with all segments of the agricultural and horticultural industries in dealing with the developing problems associated both with these economic and environmental issues. From diagnosing immediate problems to the long-range challenges of land use, environmental protection, economic viability, and health concerns, staff have worked through a network of growers, agencies and residents to help solve problems to keep Suffolk County first in agriculture in New York State and Long Island an excellent and safe place to live and work.

6. Cornell Cooperative Extension has played, and continues to play, a critical role in the development of new and expanding agricultural industries. A prime example is the local grape and wine industry which has drawn a great deal of attention, stimulated the East End economy, and supported the recreation and tourism industries.

7. The Long Island Farm Bureau and Cornell Cooperative Extension have worked closely with many other organizations in promoting agriculture, open space and other programs that enhance the value of the total environment of eastern Long Island. These programs support and accentuate the value of tourism and recreation in the area.

The need exists to continue and to enhance applied research and educational programs for all commercial farmers, agricultural businesses, elected officials, civic leaders, public employees, homeowners and residents in the area.

The IPM program is well-established as an approach to managing pests in an economically and environmentally sound manner. Because the biological system is dynamic—and, therefore, ever changing—it is essential that applied research and educational programs be current and applicable for all segments of the industry. IPM programs are developed by an IPM implementation specialist stationed at the Long Island Horticultural Research Laboratory with guidance from staff at Cornell University, local Cornell Cooperative Extension of Suffolk County staff and committees of growers utilizing the program. It is supported from Cornell and the New York State Agricultural Experiment Station at Geneva by start-up funding from the State. The cost of scouting and reporting is initially covered by the state program but is phased to private support over a three-year period.

There is a dire need to fill the Cornell Cooperative Extension associate position of entomologist at the Long Island Horticultural Research Laboratory. An additional staff technician and clerical support staff are also needed. This person would work across the fruit, vegetable, ornamental and greenhouse crops to develop management strategies for economically and environmentally important insects. The responsibilities of the entomologist position include developing productive systems and alternative control strategies, such as biological control and least-toxic pest management. This position has responsibilities in vegetable, nursery, greenhouse and fruit crops. Although based at the Long Island Horticultural Research Laboratory, the entomologist has responsibilities for the development of IPM recommendations throughout New York State.

The direction of the new IPM programs will be in the area referred to as "Urban IPM" to deal with homeowners and those individuals and businesses dealing with commercial buildings and residences.

The current weed science specialist on staff of Cornell Cooperative Extension of Suffolk County is funded with Smith Lever funds through the Director's Office at Cornell University. The position carries statewide responsibilities for applied research and Cornell Cooperative Extension education programs in lawn, garden and ornamental and some fruit and vegetable weed control. Major emphasis has been on understanding weed competition and growth with results aimed at alternative control methods. The position is assigned to Long Island because nearly one-half of all horticultural crop production in New York State is grown on Long Island and because the need for information by homeowners and horticultural businesses is more critical here. The use of herbicides (weed control chemicals) accounts for the greatest segment of pesticide chemical use by both homeowners and commercial users.

There is a continuing need to encourage progressive businesses to develop new crops, new cultural methods and new marketing techniques in all segments of agriculture. In the past, the New York State Department of Agriculture and Markets provided grants through their Agricultural Research and Development Program to producers to do such things as purchase grafted dwarfing rootstocks on sweet cherries to encourage a pick-your-own planting. This statewide program allocated $3,822,000 from FY85-86 through FY90-91. In FY90-91, $500,000 was allocated for this effort.

As we enter the next phase of the Controlled Environment Agriculture, it will be important to include eastern Long Island as a demonstration site because of the concentration of greenhouse production. Suffolk County has almost 50% of the greenhouse production in New York State. On-site managers are to be trained in the latest techniques of modern production and progress monitored by Cornell Cooperative Extension staff so that information can be passed on to other participants.

Proposed Action by the Governor:

THE FOLLOWING recommendations are made to support the applied research and Extension efforts on Long Island:

1. If successful, the effort to update the formula for allocation of funds for County Law 224 would allow Cornell Cooperative Extension of both Nassau and Suffolk Counties to receive a more equitable share of funds based on local support. The intent of County Law 224 was to provide matching funds in relationship to the county appropriations. Currently, Cornell Cooperative Extension of Suffolk County is receiving about $45,000 under the state formula. The new formula would provide 50 cents on the dollar for the first $100,000 and 5 cents on the dollar on appropriations over $100,000. Based on the proposed formula, there would be an increase of about $109,000.

2. New York State should continue to support the Integrated Pest Management (IPM) program through Cornell University's College of

Agriculture and Life Sciences. The IPM Implementation Specialist position must be continued.

3. The Extension Entomology positions and the Weed Science specialist positions should be funded through New York State County Law 224B (Assembly Bill #8679, signed by the Governor on July 17, 1989, Chapter 575, Laws of 1989). Cornell Cooperative Extension of Suffolk County would be the recipient of these funds in support of the Long Island area entomology and weed science programs stationed at the Long Island Horticultural Research Laboratory. Staff in both positions would conduct applied research at the Long Island Horticultural Research Laboratory in cooperation with commercial firms in close cooperation with other Extension Agents and with the East End towns but with information and educational programs applicable to all towns in Nassau and Suffolk Counties.

4. The New York State Department of Agriculture and Markets Innovative Grants program should be restored to previous funding levels to encourage new and adapted production or marketing techniques.

Recommendation #4:

MORE AGRICULTURAL PARCELS SHOULD BE ELIGIBLE FOR AGRICULTURAL ASSESSMENT

Background

WE SUPPORT S 4654 (Kuhl, et al.; attached as Appendix A), a bill that allows farmers with less than ten acres but with at least $50,000 in gross annual sales to qualify for agricultural assessment. There are many viable agricultural operations in the state with significant annual gross sales of products; however, they are not currently eligible for the agricultural assessment program because their operation consists of less than ten acres. This is particularly true among the greenhouse industry which produces significant amounts of agricultural products, but in many situations, on less than ten acres of farmland.

Typically, greenhouse operators have several acres of land producing fresh vegetables, nursery stock, flowers, or other agricultural commodities. However, there are numerous instances where the accompanying land does not reach the ten-acre threshold for eligibility. Often, the land has tremendous development value associated with it because of its desirable location along a commercial corridor or near large residential populations. While greenhouse growers need to keep this land in production as part of their overall operation, they cannot afford the property taxes at exorbitantly high full-value assessment levels. As a result, much of this land is converted to a non-farm use.

S 4654 would justifiably extend the agricultural assessment provisions to agricultural enterprises badly in need of the beneficial tax benefits associated with the Agricultural Districts Law. If these types of operations are made eligible, a significant amount of farmland in areas facing extreme development pressures would receive much needed property tax relief.

In addition, a mechanism should be developed in the state aid to education formula to avoid penalizing municipalities which encourage this type of agricultural assessment.

Proposed Action by the Governor:

THE GOVERNOR SHOULD introduce and/or support the substance of S 4654 to make eligible for agricultural assessment farm parcels of less than 10 acres but with gross revenues of $50,000 or more.

Passage of this legislation would further the declared policy of the state to protect agricultural lands. Farmland protection goals will be significantly advanced, particularly, in those parts of the state where the remaining farmland base is rapidly diminishing, such as the East End.

Recommendation #5:

HORSE BOARDING OPERATIONS SHOULD BE ELIGIBLE FOR AGRICULTURAL ASSESSMENT

Background

WE SUPPORT A 4806 (Parment, et al.; attached as Appendix B), a bill that would allow certain horse boarding operations to qualify for the agricultural assessment provisions of the Agricultural Districts Law. Specifically, Section 301 definitions would be amended to include horse boarding.

It is important to note that in order to qualify for an agricultural assessment, land used in agricultural production means not less than ten acres of land used as a single operation in the preceding two years must produce an average gross sales value of $10,000 or more per year.

Currently, horse *breeding* operations qualify for the agricultural assessment program. This has helped horse farmers across the state keep their land in agriculture due to the property tax benefits provided by the agricultural assessment. Because of the high development value on much of the open farmland in eastern Suffolk County, many farmers cannot afford to pay the property taxes at full value.

We believe that horse *boarding* operations provide numerous benefits to the East End by enhancing the rural character of the area, providing scenic vistas, maintaining open space, and providing recreational opportunities to support tourism.

Many horse boarding operations are experiencing extreme development pressures and high property taxes. We believe New York State should encourage horse boarding operations to avoid the conversion of farmland to development uses. This legislation would bring much needed relief to the horse industry. Consequently, valuable farmland will remain in agriculture, thereby ensuring the quality of life for our residents.

In addition, a mechanism should be developed in the State aid to education formula to avoid penalizing municipalities which encourage this type of agricultural assessment.

Proposed Action by the Governor:

THE GOVERNOR SHOULD introduce and/or support A 4806 to allow horse boarding to qualify for agricultural assessment.

Recommendation #6:

A "GROWN ON LONG ISLAND" CAMPAIGN SHOULD BE PROMOTED

Background

IN 1985, Long Island Farm Bureau and Suffolk County Industrial Development Agency sponsored a "Grown on Long Island" Logo Contest. Over 200 entries were judged by the Suffolk County Agricultural Advisory Board. Enclosed is a reproduction of the winning selection.

The "Grown on Long Island" contest was held to heighten public awareness of Long Island's rich agricultural tradition and, at the same time, develop a trademark to identify our top-quality, Long Island-grown products.

Our agricultural heritage continues to thrive in Eastern Suffolk County despite difficult economic pressure, which is indicative of the industry's importance and level of regional pride. The "Grown on Long Island" logo is now used by 100 individual growers of agricultural products to foster the image of Long Island's quality products and attempt to change consumers' attitudes in supporting our regional resources.

The "Grown on Long Island" effort compliments the developing agri-tourism industry on Long Island. In general terms, an agri-tourism enterprise is a business conducted by a farm operator for the enjoyment and education of the public and to *promote* the products of the farm thereby generating additional farm income. Agri-tourism spans a wide range of recreational and hospitality businesses including, but not limited to, farm tours, bed-and-breakfasts, wineries, petting zoos, hunting and fishing, horseback riding, hayrides, farm-based cross-country skiing, and camping. Successful agri-tourism enterprises may exist with other retail operations on the farm such as farm stands, pick-your-own operations, craft shops or other related revenue generating activities.

A growing number of U-Pick and Farm Market operators are establishing related activities including hay and sleigh rides, pumpkin picking, and haunted houses, as well as demonstrations, such as apple-cider pressing, maple syrup production, sheep shearing, etc. These are creative means to enhance tourists' visiting experience and encourage them to buy local farm products.

Agri-tourism offers benefits to the family farm and community at large. The farmer and family benefit by the direct financial contribution to the farm operation which enhances farm profitability. Agri-tourism ends the isolation of farmers by strengthening the farmers' ties to the community. Additionally, the public has the opportunity to better understand what agriculture is really about.

Proposed Action by the Governor:

WE URGE THE Governor to:

1. Direct Department of Economic Development to include matching grants for the program "Grown on Long Island" ($50,000 per year from the state to be matched by industry, i.e., Long Island Farm Bureau).

2. Personally do a "Grown on Long Island" promotional spot on Long Island and New York media to promote Long Island region in conjunction with "I Love New York" ads or Seal of Quality.

3. Direct the New York state Department Economic Development and New York Ag & Markets to promote agri-tourism and to further develop and distribute a regional catalog of existing farmstands, U-Pick operations, wineries, garden centers, farm tours and other recreational opportunities for visitors to Long Island in cooperation with industry.

FISHING INDUSTRY

Overview

FISHING INDUSTRY

LARRY CANTWELL
Commissioner, Atlantic State Marine Fisheries Commission

THE FISHING INDUSTRY, both recreational and commercial, is the backbone of the East End's economy. The industry is diverse and its water-dependent businesses include baymen, ocean-going trawlers, seafood stores, tackle shops, marinas, charter boats, and the many components of the small businesses that are the job generators of our nation's economy.

The annual dockside value of commercial landings in New York State is $54 million (*see*, Appendix C) which generates $230 million of economic activity, the vast majority of which is on the East End. There are over 29,000 people and businesses directly employed in the seafood industry of New York.

The largest port on the East End is Montauk which exceeds Boston in landings of fish, followed by Shinnecock and Greenport. Fifteen million pounds of seafood are landed at Montauk per year and ten million pounds at Shinnecock.

The East End is a primary resort destination for the 500,000 households in the Long Island-Metropolitan area that participate in marine recreational fishing. It is estimated that recreational fishing in the State generates $1 billion in expenditures to the State's economy. The contribution that this activity makes in real dollars to East End tourism is very significant.

There are a number of opportunities for economic growth in the fishing industry. International markets exist for fish populations available to East End fishermen. Certain species, such as mackerel and dogfish, are underutilized and in relative abundance (*see*, Appendix D). Markets exist for such species, particularly for export to European countries, but the lack of onshore facilities for cleaning, freezing, and packaging does not allow New York's fishermen to compete in these markets.

East End fishermen and the businesses they support must also compete with other states. For example, commercial fishing vessels that are home ported on the East End travel to Rhode Island for fuel because Rhode Island exempts them from state taxes on fuel at the pump, while in New York, the exemption is limited to a reimbursement basis. *New York, therefore, loses millions of dollars in fuel sales along with marine supply sales.* This inequity should be resolved through legislation in New York if not possible by administrative action.

The charter boat businesses compete with New Jersey and New England recreational fishing ports for tourism dollars. This industry needs the support of New York State's tourism promotional efforts in order to compete as well.

The health of both recreational and commercial fishing is forever dependent on the marine environment and any effort to support fishing must begin with the protection of the marine habitat. The devastating effects on fishing— and, in particular, shellfishing of the brown tide—are well documented. The "Brown Tide Comprehensive Assessment and Management Program" is a good starting point from which governments on every level should launch programs of protection and remediation. The Town of Southampton has passed a $2 million bond issue for a storm water run-off abatement program. All other East End towns have identified critical areas where run-off is a problem and started remediation programs. New York State highways are also a cause of concern to the water quality of the Peconic Bay system, and the New York State Department of Transportation should begin a stormwater run-off remediation program.

The focus of our recommendations for the fishing industry fall into three basic categories: environmental protection of marine habitat and water quality, regulatory changes that allow New York's fishermen to compete in the international marketplace, and incentives to attract capital investment in plant and equipment for shoreside support facilities.

Recommendation #7:

A PROGRAM OF STORMWATER RUN-OFF REMEDIATION, LAND USE CONTROL, AND STRATEGIC LAND ACQUISITIONS SHOULD BE CARRIED OUT BY LOCAL, COUNTY AND STATE GOVERNMENTS IN THE PECONIC BAY ESTUARY AREA

Background

THE EAST END of Long Island's marine waters are incurring impacts from a wide range of point and non-point sources. Increasing underwater acreage is becoming uncertified or conditionally certified for shellfish harvest because of increased coliform bacteria counts. The Nassau-Suffolk Regional Planning Board's 208 Study concluded that over 90% of the bacteria-related shellfish closures are due to stormwater run-off. The County's Brown Tide Comprehensive Assessment and Management Program identified stormwater run-off as the largest and most significant source of total and fecal coliform loading to the Peconic River and Flanders Bay (*see*, Appendix E). The impacts of pollutants and brown tide have devastated the East End's shellfish industry. In 1982, bay scallop catches accounted for 28% of the entire United States landings and had a dockside landing value of $7.3 million (1982 dollars). After the onset of brown tide, the landings have fallen as low as 300 pounds per year. In addition, the oyster industry—once worth $3.4 million in 1982—has plummeted to as little as $10,000 pear year.

The inclusion of the Peconic Bay into the National Estuary Program[1] and Moriches and Shinnecock bays into the New York State South Shore Estuary Reserve present excellent opportunities to address water quality degradation in local waters. While the State's commitment has been helpful, County and local government see the State's role in abating water pollution as critical, largely because of the State road systems which drain into the bays and harbors of the East End. Moreover, the County Brown Tide Comprehensive Assessment & Management Plan makes a policy declaration of no-net nitrogen increase in county waters. Affirmative state action is essential to meet this objective.

---

[1]The Peconic Bay is one of only 20 bays in the country to have received this designation. This program is part of the Federal Clean Water Act of 1987.

An example of the effectiveness of a program of stormwater remediation is the Town of Southampton's remediation project at Fish Cove. Fish Cove is an enclosed tidal cove that had been closed to shellfish harvesting because of pollution and excessive fecal coliform levels. Southampton invested $50,000 to install leaching pools and recharge basins and mitigated direct discharge into the marine waters. Two years later, water quality improved, Fish Cove was conditionally opened for shellfish harvesting, and over one million shellfish have been safely harvested in the past year. As a result of this success, Southampton Town has passed a $2 million bond issue to carry out a Town-wide program (*see*, Appendix F).

The real economic cost of a decline in our marine habitat must be measured against more than the loss of certain shellfish industries because the loss to consumers, seafood businesses, and tourism all have a significant negative impact on the East End's economy.

Marine habitat protection should qualify for funding under the New York State Environmental Protection Act. The preservation of wetlands along the Peconic Bay Estuary system should be a priority . Matching funds from the Environmental Protection Act should be used for both wetlands acquisition and stormwater remediation projects.

Proposed Action by the Governor:

1. The State Department of Transportation should be directed to undertake a comprehensive review of its highway system on the East End in order to identify areas where road run-off and drainage systems are sources of pollution. A road run-off remediation project should thereafter be funded by the State to correct any run-off from State roads that is contributing to water quality degradation.

2. The Department of Environmental Conservation should be directed to work with each town on the East End to establish a priority list of land acquisitions targeted for wetlands protection.

3. Marine habitat protection should qualify for funding under the New York State Environmental Protection Act. The preservation of wetlands along the Peconic Bay Estuary system should be a priority and matching funds from the Environmental Protection Act should be used for both wetlands acquisition and stormwater remediation projects.

4. Cornell Cooperative Extension's wetlands initiative should be funded. County Law 224B, passed in 1989, is the legislative framework for funding of this program. Funding would be used to employ a wetlands resource specialist with support in the amount of $45,000.

Recommendation #8:

AN OYSTER MARICULTURE TRAINING PROGRAM FOR EASTERN LONG ISLAND COMMERCIAL FISHERMEN SHOULD BE CREATED

Background

THE OBJECTIVES OF THIS project are to get commercial fishermen involved in a two-year mariculture project to supplement their incomes without risking large amounts of capital; to use currently under-utilized submerged lands under public (State, Suffolk County or local) or private control; and to create "success stories" that will encourage further the farming of shellfish in New York State waters.

Oyster culture has been practiced in New York State since the 1800's. At first, seed oysters were brought in from nursery areas in New York and Connecticut and grown out on large tracts of underwater land. More recently (1960's), oyster hatcheries have provided seed for public and private mariculture operations.

While municipal programs have been expanded in the last ten years, the number of private ventures has stagnated and even declined. Resistance from commercial harvesters opposed to private use of large tracts of public underwater land is one reason why new mariculture start-ups have been few in the last decade. In 1987, the State of Florida initiated a program to retrain oyster harvesters to culture oysters. The Harbor Branch Oceanographic Institution along with the State of Florida, U.S. Department of Labor and the Office of the Governor cooperated on the project. Results are encouraging and can be applied to New York State.

New York currently has 160 square miles of public and private underwater land in the Peconic and Gardiners Bay system. Much of this area was once used for oyster seed growout, and could once again be utilized. Rather than having a few large companies lease large tracts from the state and county, smaller areas (two to five acres) could be put aside for local commercial fishermen to try their hand at oyster farming. Seed would be procured from public and private hatcheries in New York. In 1991, the oyster harvest (farmed and wild-caught) was worth $2.7 million. Oysters are known to be fast-growing and highly valued—a perfect mariculture species. While there are risks to any farming operation, the benefits should outweigh them over time.

In order to foster mariculture development in New York State, success stories are needed. The project proposed here has the potential to produce twenty of them. These stories would be told by extension professionals and, more importantly, by the fishermen themselves, almost guaranteeing adoption by others.

The potential for oyster growout on a small-scale or a "cottage industry" approach is great. For example, an investment of $2,500 could provide an income of $20,000 over two years on less than two acres.

Inshore commercial fisherman or "baymen" are well-equipped to carry out a project of this kind. They have the skills, tools and work ethic necessary to farm oysters. All they need in addition to these traits is some technical training, financial help and supervision for the first few years. After that, the project should be self-sustaining, with additional baymen becoming involved over time.

Fishermen from the five East End towns will be asked (through their associations) if they would like to participate in the program. Up to twenty will be able to participate under this proposal. Training sessions will be held over the winter, where participants will learn about the life cycle of the oyster, methods of culture and the "belt" system to be used in this program. Materials will be provided and each participant will be required to make up a belt system over the winter/early spring (see attached budget).

Participants will be expected to provide their own workboats and fuel as well as labor to construct, deploy, maintain and harvest the belt system. In May-June of each year, up to 50,000 oyster seed at 6 millimeters (quarter inch) will be provided to each culturist. Cornell Cooperative Extension personnel will assist in stocking the system initially and help in record-keeping.

It is possible that after two to three growing seasons, oysters will be marketable, with high survival likely due to protection from predation. Culturists would be able to ask a high price for their product due to its high quality and the ability to "wait out" the market.

At the end of each year, a detailed report will be prepared and a presentation made at the Long Island Fishermen's Forum. It is expected that these sessions will generate interest in the project by non-participants, perhaps encouraging them to start up a similar operation on their own. At the end of the project, a 15-20 minute broadcast-quality video and companion publication will be produced about all facets of the project. This video will be made available through the lending libraries of Cornell Cooperative Extension and others as appropriate.

Proposed Action by the Governor:

THE GOVERNOR SHOULD fund a two-year mariculture training program on the East End.

The Governor should include funding for this demonstration project in the executive budget for the Department of Economic Development.

Budget:
Year One:

Belt system components 4,500 bags @ $3.50	$15,750.00
Lines, closures, spacers, anchors	$ 1,500.00
Oyster seed (one million 6 mm @ $10/thousand)	$10,000.00
Work raft to be used by participants	$ 5,000.00
Training program (course materials, instructor fee)	$ 4,500.00
Permit fees	$ 500.00
Travel (local/Florida)	$ 2,000.00
Subtotal	$39,250.00
Administrative overhead (15%)	$ 5,887.50
Year One Total	**$47,137.50**

Year Two:

Belt system components 4,500 bags @ $3.50	$15,750.00
Lines, closures, spacers, anchors	$ 1,500.00
Oyster seed (one million 6 mm @ $10/thousand)	$10,000.00
Permit fees (renewal)	$ 500.00
Travel (local)	$ 500.00
Video/publication production	$ 5,000.00
Subtotal	$33,250.00
Administrative overhead (15%)	$ 4,987.50
Year Two Total	**$37,637.50**
Total project cost (years One and Two)	**$82,775.00**

Recommendation #9:

A FUNDING PROGRAM TO FINANCE FISH PROCESSING FACILITIES SHOULD BE DEVELOPED

Background

DURING THE 1980'S, the state established a Striped Bass Fishermen's Emergency Assistance Program and a Commercial Fisheries Economic Assistance Program to aid the New York State fishermen of Eastern Long Island. The purpose of that program was to overcome the severe economic conditions resulting from the ban on striped bass fishing and the deterioration of the scallop industry heavily damaged by brown tide.

These two programs, funded by $350,000 from the Urban Development Corporation (UDC) and $200,000 from the New York State Department of Environmental Conservation, were combined into the Fishermen's Assistance Fund administered by the Job Development Authority (JDA) in consultation with a Fisheries Loan Advisory Committee and with the assistance of Cornell Cooperative Extension of Suffolk County/Marine Program. The program continues to provide loans to fishermen to expand current fishing activities, or to develop non-fisheries related enterprises. No application or closing fees are charged to borrowers. The interest rate is 3%. We propose an extension of these programs as follows:

Proposed Fisheries Shoreside and Infrastructure Development Assistance Program Overview:

THE GOVERNOR'S EAST END Task Force on fisheries has identified the need for specific assistance to support fisheries shoreside infrastructure development. New York's seafood industry is almost exclusively a freshfish and shellfish business. The lack of shoreside processing is a severe limitation in our industry's ability to compete, especially in the international market place. There is little, if any, market in the United States for certain species of fish, such as dogfish, despite their relative abundance. However, European and Asian markets exist for certain underutilized species of fish but require shoreside processing, packaging, and transportation that are lacking in New York (*see*, Appendix G). This proposal involves converting the very successful economic assistance program for fishermen into a program that would focus on fisheries shoreside and infrastructure development needs.

While not all of those commercial fishermen affected by either the striped bass closure or the bay scallop collapse received assistance, the revolving loan program (and the accumulated funds) create an opportunity to address the shoreside needs of the commercial fishing industry.

Because of all the negative impacts on the industry (pollution, overfishing, user conflicts, fisheries management, economic uncertainty), the future of fisheries development will depend on unique and creative initiatives to shoreside processing, marketing and distribution

More importantly, a related and real concern involves continuing to assist entry or expansion into existing competitive fisheries. Accordingly, Phase III of the Fisheries Development Program identifies the focus on the continuation of providing financial assistance for fisheries shoreside and infrastructure development purposes.

Project scope involves factors such as the entire project size, which includes total dollars, number of people involved, number of participants, number of cooperating enterprises, spin-off impacts, as well as local and regional significance. Items of importance would include multi-funding combinations such as participant capital, bank and other assistance. Programs involving interpretation of harvest, processing, marketing and distribution that represent qualitative project scope impacts, as would partnership efforts to form marketing cooperatives and joint ventures. Funding should be expanded from the existing $550,000 base to a $5 million revolving loan program. In addition, the State could assist by organizing a consortium of banks with State guarantees to fund part of this program.

Project Feasibility:

PROPOSED PROJECTS SHOULD include economic projections and descriptions of the project activities relative to available aquatic resource marketing opportunities, competition, and identify any restraints or barriers to successful endeavors. Specific requirements could include a five-year income projection, as well as a project financial statement and other information that may be requested.

Project Limits:

BECAUSE OF THE NATURE of a revolving loan, applicants should be awarded on the basis of availability of funds. A maximum loan total should be established—a suggested level would be $1,000,000.

Applicant Eligibility:

1. Proposals for funding should be accepted from applicants with a minimum of three years active and immediate experience as demonstrated through records that include federal tax returns, quantitative descriptions of existing and previous experience, income and feasibility projections, and other information that may be requested.

2. Applicants must demonstrate a proven ability to carry out all elements of the proposed project.

3. Special consideration will be given to applicants who have been impacted by any negative environmental or resource impacts, such as the brown tide, bay scallop collapse, water decertification, as well as any state or federal fisheries management action that may preclude or limit their ability to continue in the present fishery operation as long as they can meet requirements 1 and 2.

Project Examples:

1. The Suffolk Seafood Company has a sales agreement to export market 1.5 million pounds of dogfish (undermarketed species) to Germany. In order to process dogfish and meet product demands, Suffolk Seafoods needs to purchase additional equipment. In addition, Suffolk Seafoods has bid on a state contract to supply seafood for correctional institutions (*see*, Appendix H).

Skinning/Cutting Machine	$150,000
IQF/Freezer	75,000
	$225,000

Projected gross sales revenue for both sales opportunities are $2.5 million in annual sales. Gross profits before taxes on fisheries-related business revenue is typically ten (10%) percent—resulting in projected before-tax income of $250,000.

2. Montauk Boatmen, a cooperative made up of charter boatmen, operates a marina and dock and sail charters. A significant cost is bait. In order to cut cost and purchase bait from local commercial fishermen, Montauk Boatmen wants to construct a bait freezer and holding building on their property. Presently, bait is purchased from out-of-state suppliers because processing and holding facilities don't exist on Eastern Long Island. Bait includes both underutilized and by-catch species such as illex squid, sand eels, herring, bunker, baitfish, etc.

Estimated building and equipment costs are $150,000.

The above two projects have applied for financial assistance from the Fisheries Shoreside and Infrastructure Funds Program.

Proposed Action by the Governor:

THE GOVERNOR SHOULD propose funding in the executive budget for the Fisheries Shoreside Development Assistance Program to be Administered by the Job Development Authority.

Recommendation #10:

SALES TAX EXEMPTION OF FUEL PURCHASES AT THE PUMP FOR COMMERCIAL FISHERMEN SHOULD BE ADOPTED

Background

FUEL DISTRIBUTORS servicing commercial fishermen are required to charge sales tax on diesel fuel purchases used by commercial fishermen. Commercial fishermen are exempt from the tax, but must pay it up front and be reimbursed through the State's Sales and Taxation Office by submitting required forms on an interim basis. The ports of Shinnecock, Montauk, Freeport and, to a lesser extent, Islip and Greenport, provide varied services for commercial fishermen. One of those services is providing fuel. This generates a sizable amount of gross economy for those facilities providing this service. However, the quantity of fuel being purchased by commercial fishermen has diminished greatly in the last several years, primarily as a result of the sales tax exemption status. Yearly, millions of gallons of fuel that were being purchased on Long Island by commercial fishermen is no longer the case, as many boats travel to various ports in New England and other areas to avoid this very expensive up-front cost. The end result is not only lost revenues to the dock facilities, but can also lead to the product being off loaded in various ports as a matter of convenience, as well as purchase of supplies and other materials. In ongoing communications over the years, the Sales and Taxation Office has maintained that the elimination of commercial fisherman having to pay the sales tax up front would create a loophole in the present law and procedure, thus creating potential loss of revenue to the State of New York by non-commercial users.

Legislation (S.1705) has been introduced by local state representatives to exempt commercial fisherman, but as of this date, no action has occurred and the proposed legislation has existed for over two years.

Proposed Action by the Governor:

1. The Governor should introduce legislation similar to Senate Bill S1705 to exempt commercial fishermen from sales tax on fuel at the pump. However, this might be accomplished by a departmental ruling since present law

provides for this exemption, but only on a reimbursement basis.

2. The Governor should introduce legislation that would define commercial party and charter boatmen as commercial users thereby making them eligible for the fuel sales tax exemption.

Recommendation #11:

UNEMPLOYMENT INSURANCE BENEFITS FOR FISHING CREW MEMBERS SHOULD NOT BE REQUIRED

Background

CREW MEMBERS ON commercial fishing vessels are treated as self-employed individuals for Social Security, federal income tax and state income tax purposes. In addition, crew members are also seen as self-employed individuals for Federal Unemployment Tax (FUTA). However, recently, on a frequent basis, several captains have been approached by the Department of Labor with Unemployment Insurance claims made against them by crew members. (Along with this claim is the added expense of paying claims made, as well as maintaining State Unemployment Insurance for existing crew members.) Ironically, very few of any commercial fishermen and fishing vessel owners pay Unemployment Insurance. Since they are of the understanding that crew members, as already mentioned, are considered self-employed individuals and, in fact, receive a 1099F income reporting statement indicating they are self-employed. Nonetheless, in several administrative hearings and other rulings made by the Department of Labor, they have ruled that crew members for Unemployment Insurance purposes within the State of New York are seen as employees and are subject to those rules and regulations. This decision defies logic and, in the words of the last administrative judge to review this matter, the only way to change this particular ruling or decision would be through a legislative process and/or from a high-level departmental decision. From what we've been able to determine, other states in the region, primarily New England and those having a commercial fishing industry, do not have a similar ruling. The basis of the State's ruling has been that the control of the individual rests in the hands of the captain, and this is one test of the employee/employer relationship which would not exempt crew members from Unemployment Insurance. Information relative to the lay system, or share system, which is used by commercial fishermen, and the fact that they are now required to have copies of the share agreement on file with the Coast Guard have also similarly been dismissed.

Proposed Action by the Governor:

THE GOVERNOR SHOULD seek from the Commissioner of the Department of Labor and other high-level officials a departmental ruling resulting in the clarification of the status of crew members as self-employed individuals for State Unemployment Insurance purposes.

Recommendation #12:

SHINNECOCK COMMERCIAL DOCK FACILITIES SHOULD BE EXPANDED

Background

THIS PROJECT CONSISTS OF construction of an additional docking facility for commercial fishing boats. The existing dock was built in 1984 by the County of Suffolk and is leased to the Town of Southampton which operates the facility. It presently provides dock space for 22 boats.

The expansion of this facility is necessary to keep up with the expanding commercial fishing industry in this specific area. Commercial fishing is now occurring much further offshore than in the past. This requires that fishing vessels be 70-85 feet in length so that they are capable of extended fishing trips. There is now a lack of docking space for these larger vessels. When more docking space is created, these commercial fishermen can upgrade their vessels to a size that can handle these extended fishing trips. In addition, the improved navigation of Shinnecock Inlet has resulted in the inlet stabilization project presently in progress by the Army Corps of Engineers, will encourage the greater utilization of this facility by local vessels, as well as transient or out-of-state vessels. It is estimated that presently the 45 vessels that are home ported at Shinnecock generate $10 million of dockside income per year. The addition of 12-15 vessels will generate an additional $2.5-$3.5 million dockside income. A State/Countywide multiplier associated with fisheries products is 4.2. This means that roughly $10,600,000-$14,800,000 would be generated within the local area as a result of the expansion of the existing facility.

Over the next five years, it is estimated that 70-90 jobs on commercial boat crews, and 30-40 jobs in boat repair, maintenance and fish processing, packing and transport industries would be created as a result of this project. The majority of these jobs would be the outgrowth of present vessel owners and crews who will expand their existing operation and upgrade their vessels. Twenty-five jobs will be created for one year, during the construction phase.

This project consists of construction of an additional docking facility for commercial boats. A preliminary estimate for the total construction cost of this project is $2 million.

The economic development activity related to the project is the expansion of an already successful commercial fishing industry at the site, which will significantly increase employment opportunities.

There presently is a request by 10 boat owners for dock space. Dock space for large boats is minimal. The new facility will enable vessel owners to expand and upgrade their operations and, at the same time, open dock space at existing facilities for smaller vessels.

Both the Town of Southampton and Suffolk County have indicated their willingness to participate in e cost of the expansion of the Shinnecock commercial fish dock.

Proposed Action by the Governor:

THE GOVERNOR SHOULD support additional funding for the Regional Economic Development Partnership Grants Program in the executive budget. The Shinnecock Dock Project could be accomplished with 50% State funding with matching funds shared between Southampton Town and Suffolk County.

Recommendation #13:

EAST END SHELLFISH RESOURCES LOCATED IN UNCERTIFIED SHELLFISHING AREAS SHOULD BE MANAGED THROUGH CONTROL PURIFICATION (DEPURATION)

Background

EASTERN LONG ISLAND includes literally hundreds, and possibly thousands of acres of shellfishing areas that are closed due to uncertified waters. History of chronic pollution suggests that these areas may not be open to shellfish in the foreseeable future. The presence of shellfish populations in these areas also makes them vulnerable to illegal harvesting and introduces the possibility that contaminated product from these uncertified areas will enter the market. It is also understood that many of these areas represent vibrant shellfish spawning and nursery habitats which foster the establishment of healthy shellfish populations. Of course, one reason that healthy shellfish populations exist is because of the limited harvesting that occurs because the area is closed to shellfishing. But, it is also evident that these areas, aside from the pollution factor, provide an environment suitable for shellfish growth.

Consequently, the same population that poses a threat to public and creates enforcement problems has the potential for alleviating some of the problems of stock depletion being experienced and, in particular, in the East End the severe impact that baymen have felt as a result of a series of negative impacts. It is the intent of this proposal to undertake a feasibility study of a management plan for uncertified areas containing shellfish resources which is aimed at reducing the inherent health hazard by providing future continued utilization of the area and resources. The actual plan involves a long-term approach to resource management which proposes to initially minimize the existing health threat. The plan will involve the utilization of uncertified areas in a way as to provide a substantial source of shellfish which will be rendered usable through a publicly operated control purification facility.

Controlled purification, also called depuration, has historically been used to cleanse shellfish which are harvested from restricted or uncertified waters. This technology can also be used to certify the quality of shellfish harvested from open or clean waters. In controlled depuration, shellfish are held on racks in a series of tanks. Marine water which has been disinfected with ultraviolet light is recirculated through the tanks. The ultraviolet light sterilizes and kills viruses and bacteria found in the process water, including potentially pathogenic ones. Shellfish being purified are held in treated water for about 48 hours. During this period of time, the shellfish metabolize as usual and purge the contents of their stomachs. After treatment, they are removed, washed, culled and packaged for sale. Each lot of shellfish is tested before and after to insure that the bacteria levels meet or exceed Interstate Sanitation Conference (ISSC) guidelines.

To determine the feasibility of establishing a shellfish management program for uncertified harvest areas for Eastern Long Island through a public controlled purification facility.

The primary purpose of the proposed project would be to determine the environmental and economic feasibility for the establishment of a public shellfish controlled purification facility. Following is a description of the scope and focus of the feasibility study.

1) Species and water quality considerations:
Development of stock assessments to provide reliable information on the dynamics of the various existing shellfish populations located in uncertified waters. This part of the program would involve a substantial amount of field investigation, primarily to determine resource availability and populations. But could include water quality work on areas where either inadequate or old information exist.

2) Preliminary blueprints and specifications for a control purification facility, including general construction consideration, control purification module, product handling equipment, laboratory construction and equipment cost analysis, and size and scale of operation.

Completion of the proposed feasibility study would enable local decision makers to determine the viability for the establishment of a publicly operated control purification facility on Eastern Long Island. The information generated will identify shellfish populations and areas, water quality related issues, and if the information generated is dealt in a positive recommendation, provide background and information from which to secure other public funding mechanisms for the establishment of this facility. A significant benefit and impact may be the determination that a substantial amount of economy and activity for baymen may be generated, providing them with the opportunity to continue to earn their living on the water. At this point, it is impossible to determine the expense associated with the proposed feasibility study, but it is estimated that the cost would not exceed $50,000; and, in fact, that number may be high depending on the availability of existing information. It is suggested that if this project is selected that a call for proposals be circulated to interested respondents.

Proposed Action by the Governor:

THE GOVERNOR SHOULD support a feasibility study of a publicly operated control purification facility on the East End. Funding in the amount of $50,000 could be made available under the State's Regional Economic Development Partnership Grant Program.

Recommendation #14:

A FISHERIES MANAGEMENT PROCESS SHOULD BE FORMALLY CREATED WITHIN DEC

Background

THE FISHING INDUSTRY operates in one of the most regulated environments of any business in the State. It is dependent on natural resources that are managed by government on many levels, not only marine fisheries, but water quality and the environment, and the forces that impact them. Because of this relationship between the regulators and regulated, there is an important need for a cooperative partnership between the State and the fishing industry. A balance must be struck between New York's responsibility to manage our public resources and the needs of fishermen to make a living from these resources.

The regulation of marine finfish and shellfish is burdened by multiple layers of government, federal and state, and by its lack of a consistent regulatory process. The regulatory process includes the federally appointed Marine Fisheries Councils, the States' Atlantic Marine Fisheries Commission, Congress, National Marine Fisheries Service, U.S. Department of Commerce, New York State Legislature and the New York State Department of Environmental Conservation. This myriad of bodies and responsibilities is difficult, at best, for the most informed to understand and leaves the average fisherman in the dark.

In New York, the DEC is granted regulatory authority over certain species but not others, unlike freshwater fish where DEC has complete regulatory authority. Our belief is that fisheries management should be removed from the political process to the extent possible.

Regulatory authority should be vested with DEC and the Legislature removed from the process to the extent that it is lawful. Linked to this recommendation is that DEC be required to consult with the fishermen directly impacted by any regulation, to afford the fishermen a real opportunity to help write regulations that meet the fisheries management goal. As one fisherman said, "We understand that we will be asked to sacrifice for fisheries conservation, all we ask is that we help decide how to take our medicine."

The Marine Resources Advisory Council is intended to provide advice from citizens and industry to DEC. However, its size and organization lacks the broad-based representation of the many different user groups of fishermen. The structure of M.R.A.C. does not allow for the diverse interests of the fishing industry to be fully represented in the formulation of fisheries management regulations.

Several proposals have been put forth to reorganize fisheries management in the State. Assemblyman Thomas DeNapoli has drafted a proposal that would create a new regulatory body that would have the power to adopt fisheries management regulations (*see*, Appendix I).

The East Hampton Baymens' Association has drafted a proposal for legislation that would institutionalize a process of requiring consultation and advice from a committee of commercial fishermen (*see*, Appendix J).

Proposed Action by the Governor:

THE GOVERNOR SHOULD introduce legislation that reforms the regulatory process for fisheries management. This must include a requirement that DEC obtain the recommendations of fishermen represented by a broad-based group of the different gear and user types. Regulatory authority could be vested with DEC for all species only if a mandatory consultation and advisory process is mandated that requires DEC to work directly with fishermen who would be impacted by any new regulations.

Recommendation #15:

THE SHINNECOCK INLET EROSION PROJECT SHOULD BE COMPLETED ON AN EMERGENCY BASIS

Background

EROSION THREATENS TO cut off the only road access to the Shinnecock Dock Facility. The area of erosion is approximately 3,000 feet west of Shinnecock Inlet. The commercial fishing port at Shinnecock is New York State's second most important port where over ten million pounds of fish are landed. The loss of this road access will close this port.

This area of erosion has been identified by the Governor's Task Force on Coastal Erosion as being one of the top seven priority projects to be completed on Long Island, however, no specific erosion control or emergency protection has been planned to date. The current federal project by the Army Corps of Engineers is limited to dredging maintenance of the inlet and jetty maintenance which, ironically, may be contributing to the loss of sand along the access road. The fishermen and all property owners in the area support an elevated steel bulkhead road.

Proposed Action by the Governor:

1. The Governor must press for an immediate emergency project to protect the access road in the short term. This emergency protection should be either a sand replenishment or construction of a buried steel bulkhead road to protect the access. Because of the possible connection between the inlet work and the erosion of the access road, it may be that Army Corps of Engineers should be responsible to carry out this project.

2. The long-term solution for both the maintenance of the inlet and the access road is a permanent sand bypass system which the Governor should request the Army Corps to complete.

Recommendation #16:

AQUACULTURE SHOULD BE SUPPORTED

Background

MARINE CULTURE WORK and especially shellfish culture has had a long history on the East End of Long Island. Unfortunately, many of these efforts have passed from the scene due to, among other things, their large scales, the impacts of diseases and brown tide, seed stock unreliability and the temptations of rising property values. In more recent years, some of the large shellfish companies, including Long Island Oyster Farms and Shelter Island Oyster Company, invested in hatchery operations for the production of seed but never attained the levels of commitment necessary to stave off failure.

Research into marine culture in shellfish and finfish was conducted at the former New York Ocean Science Lab in Montauk and, to a lesser extent, Suffolk County Community College Marine Center in Southold and Southampton College. Modest efforts survive at Southampton and have been replaced in Southold by Suffolk County Cooperative Extensions's Suffolk Marine Environmental Learning Center and in Montauk by The Montauk marine Science Institute. At least one private culture and live animal marketing operation, Multi Aquaculture Systems of Amagansett, was spawned by these research activities.

Ambitious projects claiming to be moving towards large-scale production of indigenous species have been reported on lately, but as yet, seem to be in the planning stages.

By and large, the current trend in active culture on the East End is in the modestly scaled production of mollusks and shellfish in the private and public sectors.

Small, private efforts have been difficult to establish due to the unavailability of prime shellfish bottom and resistance by competing interests, primarily in the traditional fishery. Successful, small operations exist on Fishers Island at the Clam Farm and Ocean Pond Corp., in part, due to the unique character of that island and its relative lack of importance to the larger traditional shellfish industry. However, grow-out of product is either completed using off-bottom techniques or by arrangement with New England growers with the advantage of leased or privately owned bottom land. A few operations on the North Fork are experimenting with land based grow-out systems, again, to avoid conflict with competing interests. There also have been a smattering of operators that have taken advantage of State assignments on which to conduct off-bottom operations, but the more successful have primarily been oriented toward relaying shellfish for depuration purposes rather than culture work per se.

Three private shellfish hatcheries operate on the East End. Two are the aforementioned Claim Farm and Ocean Pond Corp. on Fishers Island and the third is The Shinnecock Tribal Oyster Project in Southampton.

In addition to market grow-out in the case of The Clam Farm and grow-out for tribal use in the case of Shinnecock, these two hatcheries also produce seed for sale. A major market for this seed and, in fact, a premise on which the Shinnecock Project was funded, is in sales to municipalities in the region which operate restocking programs for the traditional shellfishery.

The public effort put into the enhancement of public shellfish stocks has been a major part of the marine culture activity on the East End in recent years and is in keeping with undertakings in traditional shellfish producing areas from the Canadian Maritimes to Florida. Every town has, in some way, participated in efforts to either cultivate bottom land, seed with hatchery-raised product, perform limited grow-out of hatchery product prior to seeding, or become full producers, operating their own program from hatching to stocking. East Hampton Town operates the most ambitious program producing over 10 million oysters, clams and scallops in a hatchery in Montauk begun in 1989 with the help of a grant from New York State. This hatchery, free of brown tide and operated with ever-increasing success since 1990, also devotes 10% of its production to State waters, primarily in the Eastern Peconic-Gardiners Bay system. It has also, for the past two years, been the sole source of seed scallops for important research being conducted by SUNY Stony Brook involving effects of the brown tide. The Town of Southold also operates a small hatchery with the cooperation of Suffolk County Cooperative Extension Marine Program at Suffolk Marine Environmental Learning Center in Southold. Shelter Island has participated in bottom cultivation and stocking programs also with the help of Cooperative Extension. The Towns of Riverhead and Southampton operate field grow-out programs prior to stocking and Southampton has plans to initiate a land-based grow-out system as well.

In addition to these town-wide efforts, a baymen-sponsored organization, The Long Island Greenseal Committee, with State funding, has been active in past years in bay scallop restocking efforts.

Assessments by both private and public culturists have established that oyster seed stocking is a prime contributor to harvest success. Genetic research with local bay scallops has indicated that a significant contribution has been made by introduced stocks toward sustaining a reproducing population through the worst of the brown tide period. Clam stock enhancement, while more difficult to assess, is increasing in popularity with both private and public stocking programs throughout the region.

The mistrust that has existed between the traditional fishery and culture efforts could, in the long run, damage both participants and seems to warrant an attempt at rectification. A small pilot scale demonstration project in which individual baymen were given the tools and guidance necessary to accomplish oyster grow-out from spat to market-size might make inroads into changing some attitudes within an industry struggling to survive. Existing educational programs, such as Suffolk County Cooperative Extension and area public hatcheries, could be utilized to provide the guidance and seed stocks. Sensitivity would be needed in the implementation of such a program in order to avoid the perception of abandoning the traditional fishery.

The decimation of the scallop industry as a result of the brown tide and the positive results stocking programs have had in maintaining the reproducing populations would make expansion of those efforts an effective contribution to the public resource. With modest modifications to nursery and field grow-out systems, the East Hampton Shellfish Hatchery could expand its relationship with New York State and build on its success in scallop production to make a larger contribution to area resources. In fact, at the suggestion of the Department of Environmental Conservation, Congressman Thomas Manton has proposed federal appropriations through the National Marine Fisheries Service for extended support of bay scallop restoration work on the East End. Deputy Commissioner Robert Bendick has indicated that the hatchery could be a candidate for funding under such a program. A State commitment at this time would dovetail nicely with this effort leading to compound benefits to this valuable resource.

Proposed Action by the Governor:

THE GOVERNOR SHOULD seek the support of New York's Congressional delegation and U.S. Senators for Congressman Manton's effort to secure appropriations for extended support of Bay Scallop restoration. The Agricultural Research and Development Grant Program of the Department of Agriculture and Markets should be expanded to include funds for aquaculture development on the East End.

Recommendation #17:

NEW YORK SEAFOOD COUNCIL MARKETING AND PROMOTIONAL EFFORTS SHOULD BE SUPPORTED BY A PERMANENT FUNDING MECHANISM

Background

NEW YORK'S SEAFOOD COUNCIL (NYSC) (incorporated in 1990 as a not-for-profit 501(c) corporation) is the marketing and promotion organization for New York's seafood industry. Its members include baymen, fishermen, lobstermen, wholesalers, shellfish dealers, processors, retailers, restaurants and party and charter boat operators. In addition to its marketing efforts, NYSC has played in increasingly important role by serving as a communication link between governmental and other agencies and individual sectors of the seafood industry.

NYSC has derived its present and past funding through a combination of funding and membership fees. In 1990, with the aid of a UDC/REDS grant administrated by Cornell Cooperative Extension and with the technical assistance of New York Sea Grant, NYSC initiated a quality assurance demonstration project. This project used principals of HACCP (Hazard Analysis Critical Control Points) which are likely to be the basis of future safety and inspection programs for the seafood industry. Our initiative attracted national attention and members of our organization were invited to participate in the national FDA/NOAA pilot program. Our efforts and involvement will be a continuing priority.

In 1991, NYSC received funding through the New York State Department of Agriculture & Markets to develop and initiate a Marketing and Promotional Outreach program. NYSC successfully developed the theme for its continuing "Long Island Fresh" marketing campaign and distributed over 1,500 theme posters to members and retail seafood markets. In November, 1992, with funding from a New York State Department of Economic Development Networks program, NYSC sponsored an "Export Workshop" that was attended by over 40 businesses and an impressive combination of governmental and private agencies to present the nuts and bolts of exporting seafood products. In the spring of 1993, the "Long Island Fresh" campaign was continued and expanded. In addition, the Council developed a complete data base of over 14,000 known licensed and permitted individuals and businesses involved in the harvesting, processing or sale of New York's seafood products; the Council plans to actively maintain this list.

New York's Seafood Council has been successful in beginning to define the economic importance of marketing and promotion to New York's seafood industry. As is apparent from our limited history, the potential for the NYSC to provide a significant role in marketing, promotion, education and communication is clear. As twelve other states that have seafood industries have learned, a seafood industry needs a state council. While the continuity of the Council is currently dependent upon dedicated volunteers and the ability to secure funding for specific projects, it is time to establish a secure funding mechanism that will allow a permanent organization to exist. It has been proposed that a surcharge to all licensed or permitted members of the seafood industry of New York become the basis of that funding.

Proposed Action by the Governor:

THE GOVERNOR SHOULD introduce legislation to amend State Finance Law to allow for the annual funding of a seafood industry organization, such as The Seafood Council.

WINERY INDUSTRY

Overview

WINERY INDUSTRY

CAROL GRISTINA
Owner
Gristina Vineyards

ALICE WISE
Viticulturist
Cornell Cooperative Extension

With the first winegrape vineyards planted only 20 years ago, Long Island has quickly evolved from a fledgling industry to a critically acclaimed wine region. Unlike other wine regions in New York, Long Island grows only vinifera varieties, the classic European wine grape varieties. The great wines of France, Italy and California are made exclusively from vinifera grapes. This commitment to growing and producing fine wine distinguishes Long Island from other eastern U.S. grape industries.

The evolution into a recognized wine industry has occurred for a number of reasons. On the East End, our unique "terroir"—well-drained, sandy, gravely, soils; adequate, but not excessive, rainfall; a long growing season with a warm fall and mild winter—permits the growing of cold tender vinifera varieties. Vinifera growing is an integral part of the evolution toward high-return, capital-intensive farming. The proximity of the East End to a major population center has also been an important advantage. Located only 70 miles from New York City, we are the "country neighbors" to one of the world's largest wine-consuming markets.

Today, 1500 acres are farmed in two federally recognized appellations: The North Fork of Long Island and The Hamptons. A majority of the acreage lies within the North Fork's "vineyard corridor" running from Cutchogue east to Peconic. Seventeen wineries produce 500,000 gallons of wine, close to 3 million bottles. With an average price of $9 per bottle, sales of $27 million generate almost $2 million in sales tax revenue. Clearly, the Long Island wine industry has helped to revitalize farming on the East End.

Winery tours, tastings and events have been a primary component of the advent of "agritourism." One winery estimates that 10,000 people visit their winery during a week in the summer. Up to 30% of wine sales occur directly through winery tasting rooms. The influx of tourists to the East End directly benefits a number of support businesses, such as restaurants and hotels. Wineries provide the ideal complement to local farmstands, enabling visitors to sample all of the East End's bounty.

Despite the relative infancy of the industry, East End wines have gained national and international recognition. By the late 1980's, Long Island had already become one of the premier wine growing regions in the country, according to *The Wine Spectator*, a leading wine industry publication. Awards and accolades continually bestowed upon Long Island wines reinforce this achievement.

One tangible measure of our success has been the inclusion of five Long Island wineries in the 1993 New York Wine Experience, sponsored by *The Wine Spectator*. At this symposium, a sophisticated panel of international judges chooses the finest producers from every major wine region in the world. These wineries participate in a gala tasting, the Critics Choice Grand Tasting. In 1993, 184 wineries were selected, with invitations extended to five Long Island wineries. Considering the global competition for an invitation, this, indeed, serves as one benchmark of our success.

Wine growing is a long-term, capital-intensive proposition. As with many agribusinesses, constant reinvestment is necessary to maintain both the vineyards and winery. Wineries on Long Island have done well because of the production of a quality product, the advent of agritourism, and the dedication of those working in the industry. Current production levels are modest, in fact, a number of businesses are examining the potential for increased production. Expansion of existing businesses and the planting of new vineyards will only occur if there is a ready source of inexpensive, quality farmland. A strong Farmland Preservation Program would enable an affordable land base to be created, stabilizing the future of agriculture on Long Island. In addition, the cost of mandatory programs, such as Worker's Compensation, must be controlled to minimize the tremendous financial burden already placed on farm businesses.

The Farm Winery Act of 1976 spurred the growth of the East End wineries by recognizing that the wine industry is, by nature, one of small agricultural businesses, usually family-owned and operated with limited staff and resources, and granted them some relief from the burdens of the post-Prohibition legislation of 1934.

The State of New York recently took significant steps to improve the business climate of our industry with the Present-Parment "omnibus mandate relief bill" which pre-empted several recommendations of the Vineyard Work Group. Key provisions will make it easier for small wineries to market their product, including more flexibility for conducting wine tastings in retail stores, at country fairs and farmers' markets. Among the regulatory relief measures is the elimination of a time-consuming and costly duplicative label approval process at both the Federal and State levels. The legislation recognizes the true nature of wine—as agriculture, as food, as tourism, as small business, as economic development. The State Liquor Authority is now required to promote the expansion and profitability of wine production and tourism; studies are to be conducted by the Office of Business Permits and Regulatory Assistance in conjunction with other agencies to explore further mandate relief measures. Promotional aspects of the bill include wine industry representation on the New York State Tourism Advisory Council. With regard to these recent changes, Governor Cuomo and the Legislature are to be congratulated for their leadership and vision.

In addition to the following specific Recommendations which appear beginning on page 56, as members of the Agricultural Committee, we support the following programs:

1. We support the initiation of a **State Farmland Preservation Program**, a program where the state, in partnership with the county and towns, purchases the development rights to agricultural land. This will ensure the preservation of open space, will help stabilize the agricultural industries that exist, and permit modest expansion of agriculture.

2. We strongly agree with the Agriculture Subcommittee concerning the **reform of the Worker's Compensation** program. Agricultural businesses are enduring disproportionate cost increases in Worker's Comp. While this program is necessary, farms cannot shoulder the burden of the spiraling costs associated with Worker's Compensation.

3. We recommend the reinstatement of funding for the **Research and Development Grants Program at the New York Department of Agriculture and Markets**. This program successfully funded the more innovative, less mainstream types of research in the past which are critical considering the nationwide shortage of research funding. Unfortunately, it was eliminated several years ago as a cost-cutting measure. Programs, such as alternative pest control methods, will develop only with the proper investment in research.

4. We recommend continued support and funding for Cornell University's **Long Island Horticultural Research Lab**, the key research facility for agriculture on Long Island. Currently, the Lab is attempting to secure funds for a cross-commodity entomology position, a position that existed at the Lab for many years but was put on hold due to Cornell's budgetary problems. This position plays a large role in helping growers to find ways to manage insect and mite problems and reduce pesticide use.

5. We recommend continued funding for the **Integrated Pest Management program**, also located at the Geneva Experiment Station. This program supports a **Regional IPM Specialist** position at the Research Lab in Riverhead. This position provides invaluable assistance and technical expertise for all agricultural commodities on Long Island. Much of the Specialist's work involves scouting programs which promote grower awareness of pest problems and enable reductions in pesticide use.

6. We recommend the **revision of County Law 224**, amending the formula for allocation of state funds to Cornell Cooperative Extension. This would allow Cornell Cooperative Extension of both Nassau and Suffolk Counties to receive a more equitable share of funds based on local support. *See*, Recommendation #3.

7. Two research/extension positions with broad responsibilities are based at the Long Island Horticultural Research Lab: the Weed Specialist, employed by Cornell Cooperative Extension, and the Extension Entomologist. These positions serve primarily Long Island, benefiting farmers as well as consumers across Long Island. They also assume a number of state-wide responsibilities. We recommend an adjustment in funding for these positions to ensure their long-term stability. We recommend **funding through the New York County Law 224B** (Assembly Bill #8679, signed by the Governor on July 17, 1989, Chapter 575, Laws of 1989). Cornell Cooperative Extension of Suffolk County and the IPM program would be the recipient of these funds.

8. We recommend continued support and funding for agricultural research and extension personnel at Cornell University, particularly, those located at the **New York State Agricultural Experiment Station at Geneva**. The Station houses faculty working on all aspects of fruit and vegetable production, including faculty members who conduct research in viticulture and enology. These positions frequently interact with the local wine industry, providing research-generated field recommendations. The relationship between Geneva researchers and the wine industry is critical to the long-term success of the wine industry.

The issues confronting the Long Island wine industry reflect the complex nature of our business. Continuing education for growers, wine makers, and sales staff remains vital to the making and selling of fine wine. Research is essential to address the viticultural and enological concerns of our unique wine region. Promotion of our product must grow and evolve as our industry evolves. The preservation of agriculture through farmland preservation programs and funding for support agencies must be in place. Finally, a number of legislative issues must be addressed to facilitate the running of our businesses.

These issues are central to the long-term economic viability of the Long Island wine industry. The following pages detail our recommendations.

Recommendation #18:

A VITICULTURE CONFERENCE SHOULD BE HELD ON THE EAST END

Background

IN 1988, the wine growers of Eastern Long Island held the Maritime Wine Growing Symposium, at which invited guests from the Bordeaux region of France shared their expertise with the more than 200 members of the East End's fledgling wine industry. The dual educational and promotional benefits derived from this conference have had a lasting impact on our industry.

Ideas, suggestions, and recommendations from visiting experts have found their way into the management of our vineyards and the making of our wines. As a result of this symposium, major changes took place in the training of vines, from high-wire (6') to low-wire (3') systems. Trellising strategies for dealing with high-vigor blocks were adapted by several growers. Visiting experts emphasized the need for careful vineyard management with good record-keeping and an eye for detail. Wine makers adopted a number of recommendations from the French, instituting changes in pH management and malolactic fermentation. Tasting wine with the French, in and of itself, was a tremendous educational experience.

The educational seminars were accompanied by wine tastings and dinners for participants and visiting experts. These events were covered extensively by national food and wine press. The resulting publicity elevated Long Island to a nationally prominent red wine region and is considered a pivotal point in the development of the East End wine industry. Suddenly, there was tremendous interest in the industry, an increase in tourism, and an accompanying increase in wine sales. This conference was not only educational in purpose, it provided enormous promotional and economic benefits.

Two additional conferences were subsequently held. The 1990 International Merlot Symposium was a slightly scaled-down version of the 1988 meeting. However, the benefits of this event have been evident in the award-winning Merlots now being produced on Long Island. In 1991, Improved Management Techniques for Long Island Vineyards was produced, inviting guests from California and New York to lecture on a series of innovative viticultural topics. Recommendations from these lectures and tours have translated into the nutrition and fertilization information now being used by a number of businesses.

These symposiums were funded by the Long Island Regional Education

Center for Economic Development, Bureau of Economic Development Coordination, and New York State Education Department. Moderate investments of time and money by these agencies made possible these three conferences. For example, a grant of $39,000 funded the Maritime Wine Growing Symposium. These agencies and the State of New York deserve our gratitude and thanks for providing the industry with significant educational and promotional opportunities. These conferences—particularly, the Maritime Wine Growing Symposium—are viewed as turning points in the success of the Long Island wine industry.

We recommend the production of a viticultural/enological symposium on Long Island, ideally held every two to three years. The dual educational and economic benefits of this proposed conference promises to be of tremendous importance to our young wine region.

For the inaugural conference, we recommend focusing on Chardonnay, the top white wine variety in the world and the most important variety in the Long Island industry. Approximately 40% of our vineyards—over 500 acres—are planted to Chardonnay. The vines grow well on Long Island and are hardy and productive. The wines are well-received by seasoned experts as well as new wine drinkers. Chardonnay is the backbone of our industry, the variety that wins awards and provides wineries with cashflow. We also have several excellent vintages that would show well in a conference scenario.

A Chardonnay conference in the mold of the Maritime Wine Growing Symposium would have a significant impact on our industry. Recognition of our Chardonnays would thrust Long Island permanently into the ranks of world-class Chardonnay producers. Wine growing is an expensive, long-term proposition, requiring constant reinvestment in all phases of the business. By improving our ability to grow, vinify, and market Chardonnay, wine growing would be more economically viable—even profitable. Naturally, these economic benefits would have a ripple effect on many other local support businesses.

Conference Organizers: An advisory committee (10-12 people) of winery owners, wine makers, vineyard managers, and Cornell representatives will supervise the activities of a paid coordinator. He/she would be responsible for implementing all decisions made by the group, working part-time for several months and full-time for 2-3 months.

Audience: The 200-plus members of the Long Island wine industry, Hudson Valley, Finger Lakes and Western New York wine industries, all members of U.S. wine industries, particularly, from eastern regions including Virginia, Maryland, Pennsylvania, Connecticut, Rhode Island and Massachusetts; wine press, restaurateurs and wine retailers.

Suggested Dates: This conference must be held during the growing season but before harvest, preferably, mid-July through mid-August. It is essential that visiting experts be permitted to assess both vine and fruit characteristics of our grapevines.

Educational Conference Format: We propose a two-to-three-day conference featuring the leading Chardonnay producers from Burgundy, Italy and California, including a local expert explaining Chardonnay management on Long Island. Viticultural topics would include clonal selection, nutritional needs, rootstocks, training and pruning, pest management, and vine management for optimal fruit quality. Wine topics of interest include determining optimal fruit quality for harvest, harvest methods and fruit handling, fermentation strategies, fining and filtering, and the use of barrels. A session dealing with marketing and promotional issues would be of great benefit to winery sales staff.

Vineyard tours for the visiting experts would be scheduled prior to the conference to provide an overview of local Chardonnay production. After the formal conference, smaller industry-only master sessions would facilitate interaction between visitors and industry members; for example, a workshop for vineyard managers examining clones and vineyard productivity, or a critical tasting for wine makers of their own Chardonnays.

Winery tasting room and sales staff should also participate in the educational process, through either a formal half-day session with several speakers or through a master class.

Events Format: Equally important to this symposium are the accompanying tastings and dinners. In addition to the educational seminars, we propose three official events:

1. A large public tasting of Chardonnay. Long Island wine makers and visiting experts bringing wine would be allowed a scheduled 15-minute session to describe and promote their Chardonnay.
2. A kick-off dinner for conference participants and wine press attended by 150-200 people.
3. A gala tasting and dinner for attendees, guests, visiting experts and the public attended by 300+ people. During the 1988 symposium, many wine retailers and distributors attended a similar event, bringing together those who grow the grapes, make the wine, market the wine, and sell the wine.

Location: The conference would be held on Long Island, either at a facility with a conference center or at Suffolk Community College. The facility must be able to host wine tastings and lunches (could be catered).

Industry Contributions: Members of the industry will host visiting experts in their homes, providing breakfast and transportation. An advisory committee of 10-12 people will oversee all aspects of the conference. Other industry members will be involved in the preparation and running of events. All participants will cover their own expenses for educational seminars and dinners. Wineries will donate eight or more cases of wine.

Funding Agencies: Past symposiums were funded by the New York State Department of Education, the Long Island Regional Education Center for Economic Development and its facilitating agency, Boces I Suffolk. Cornell Cooperative Extension of Suffolk County could also serve as a facilitating agency.

Promotional Aspects of Conference
(See, also, the section "Promotion of Long Island Wines")

BY HOSTING RESPECTED wine growers from world-famous Chardonnay regions, particularly, Burgundy, this conference lends itself well to the promotion of our wine region. Preliminary suggestions on specific promotional strategies include the following:

1. Key wine writers will be invited to all events, including the symposium, tastings and dinners. The press, at large, will be invited to the Chardonnay tasting and the gala tasting/dinner. Only the industry master sessions will be closed to the press.

2. Press coverage: press releases and encouragement of press coverage at each event. Radio and television interviews with visiting experts and key members of the industry. Press will be provided with a complete press kit prior to the conference. This will cover the history and current status of the industry, background on all speakers, agendas, and a profile on Chardonnay growing on Long Island.

3. A professional photographer will document all aspects of the symposium, providing photos for the press and providing wineries with photos for their tasting room.

4. Invitations to the Chardonnay tasting will be extended to local politicians and agencies dealing with the wine industry. Perhaps, a politician will deliver the opening remarks of the conference. Included will be town supervisors, county, state and federal legislators, Farm Bureau, Cooperative Extension and Soil Conservation Service personnel.

5. Winery tasting room and sales staff should also participate in the educational process through either a formal half-day session with several speakers or a master class.

6. A significant international wine writer would be an appropriate dinner speaker and would also draw in a member of the international wine press.

Proposed Action by the Governor:

THE GOVERNOR SHOULD direct the New York State Department of Education and/or the Department of Economic Development to produce a wine industry symposium focusing on Chardonnay with one or more Towns, if they wish to participate.

Proposed Budget for Wine Industry Conference

Expenses

Personnel

Conference coordinator	$ 8,000
8-10 speakers	
$2,500 foreign, $2,000 out-of-state, $500 in-state	20,000
Keynote speaker for gala dinner	2,000
Translation services (before, during, and after conference)	3,000
Secretarial support, part-time, 3-4 months	5,000
Subtotal, personnel	**$38,000**

Production/printing costs

Office	
Phones, faxes, copy machine, audio equipment, computer rental	4,200
Office supplies, conference supplies (name tags, folders, etc.)	2,000
Office overhead	2,500
Production/printing, general	
Meeting brochure	1,500
Press releases, information	1,000
Press kits production/distribution	2,000
Agendas/maps	1,500
Handouts	1,000
Proceedings production/printing/distribution, 250 copies	6,000
Copy service for volume work	1,000
Photography	3,000
Events	
Invitations/ticketing/return response	2,000
Advertising	
Advertising in trade journals	1,000
Local advertising of public events	2,000
Postage	3,000
Subtotal, production and printing	**$33,700**

Events and Facilities

Conference Hall	0
Coffee, pastries, two days, $15/person, 150 people	2,250
Lunch for 150 people, $20+/head/day, 2 days	3,000
Chardonnay Tasting, open to public, 200 people, food, utensils, glassware, wait staff, clean up @ $20/person cost	4,000
Industry dinner, $40/person cost, 200 people	8,000
Wine tasting/Grand dinner, $40/person cost, 300 people	12,000
Subtotal, events and facilities	**$29,250**

Total Expenses	**$100,950**

In-Kind Services by Wine Industry

Contacts, invitations to speakers	$ 1,000
Hosting of speakers in guest homes 8 speakers & spouse, 3 nights, breakfast equivalent to $150/night/couple	3,600
Airport and local transportation	2,000
Advisory committee: Group of 10-12 industry members that advise coordinator, plan conference Est. 100 hours per person, $25/hour, 10 people	25,000
Event preparation and running by other industry members	5,000
Donation of wine for lunches, wine tastings, dinners 17 wineries x 8 cases x $120/case	16,320
Industry members, conference fee 100 x $100 per person	10,000
Industry members, wine tasting and dinner fees	20,000
In-Kind Services by Wine Industry	**$82,920**

Revenue

No charge for visiting experts or wine press	0
Conference registration	
$100/person x 120 people, lunch included, 2 days	12,000
Chardonnay Tasting, open to public	
75 people @ $30/person	2,250
125 people at $15/person (conference participants)	1,875
Industry dinner, 150 people, $50/person	7,500
Gala wine tasting/dinner, 300 people total	10,500
$60/person conference participants, 120 people	7,200
$75/person general public, 100 people	7,500
Total Revenue	**$48,825**

Budget Summary

Total expenses	100,950
Less revenue	48,825
Grant requested	**$52,125**

Recommendation #19:

FUNDING FOR VINIFERA WINE AND GRAPE RESEARCH SHOULD BE INCREASED

Background

CURRENTLY, one full-time researcher, Ms. Alice Wise, is employed by Cornell Cooperative Extension of Suffolk County. Her responsibilities include applied research, production of educational meetings, grower consultation, newsletter, representing the industry to the press and the public, and acting as a liaison between professors at the New York State Agricultural Experiment Station and the Long Island wine industry.

In three years of employment, Ms. Wise has developed major research efforts in the following areas: clonal evaluation, horticultural oils for pest control, stem necrosis study, ground cover management, and organic fertilization studies. Three of these projects have received partial funding, two in 1993 from the New York Wine & Grape Foundation, and one from a fertilizer company. Total funding from grant moneys in 1993 was $11,000.

Difficulty in attaining proper funding can be attributed to two things. First, pest problems on Long Island are not common in the rest of New York State, leading to questions on the statewide significance of a pest problem. Second, for-profit companies, such as chemical and fertilizer companies, usually consider the market on Long Island too small to warrant any investment in product development or testing. Yet the research needs and concerns of the industry are real.

We have selected five research priorities which we feel are important issues for all vineyards and wineries. These issues address fruit and wine quality issues as well as economic and environmental issues.

The research priorities of the Long Island wine industry include

1) Evaluation of grapevine clones;
2) High-density planting;
3) Grapevine nutrition and fertilization;
4) Alternative pest controls; and
5) Rootstock evaluation.

Each of these topics requires a focused, long-term research effort in order to provide the industry with standards to maintain or improve quality in an economically viable fashion.

Our goal is to increase the volume of wine and grape research being done on Long Island, as outlined in the discussion section. This work must take place on Long Island due to our unique combination of soils, climate and grape varieties. Only under local conditions can complicated research issues be resolved.

1. Evaluation of grapevine clones. A trial evaluating winegrape clones (different strains of a single variety) has been initiated. Clones of Chardonnay, Merlot, and Cabernet Sauvignon have been grafted to two rootstocks and grown as own-rooted plants. Clones are profoundly influenced by soil, water and climate, so that local evaluation must be done to provide local recommendations. This trial will provide an intimate view of vine growth and productivity as well as fruit and wine quality. The high cost of plant material and shortage of desired clones and rootstocks delayed the planting of this trial, so that it will take 3 to 4 years to fully plant 2 acres of vineyard. *Project Impact*: This project will generate data on vine performance, fruit quality, and wine quality. Growers will be able to view vines firsthand and taste the wine made from different clones. This will provide growers with recommendations on clone type when blocks must be replanted. The first wave of replanting in the industry will likely occur in the next decade, coinciding with the publishing of information from this trial.

While this project has been started by Cornell viticulturist Alice Wise, the enormous cost of plant material, trellis, labor, harvest, fruit testing, and wine making must be addressed. Partial funding has been secured on a year-by-year basis, and some materials and labor have been donated, however, the size and scope of this project necessitate the securing of significant outside funding. It is currently not forthcoming.

Estimated costs, 1994: $12,000

$ 6,000	Temp. labor: maintenance and research
2,000	Soil and tissue testing
2,000	Trellis materials and installation
2,000	Supplies and materials

Estimated costs, per year, starting 1995: $32,000

$14,000	Temp. labor: maintenance, research, harvest, data entry
2,000	Supplies and materials
4,000	Soil, tissue and fruit testing
2,000	Transportation of fruit to NYS Ag. Expt. Station, Geneva
10,000	Small lot, experimental wine making, NYS Ag Expt. Station, Geneva or subsidy for local winemaking services

2. High-density planting. The density of vines in a given area is a hotly debated topic. We do know that the sandier soils of Long Island tend to grow small vines. Therefore, the traditional upstate vine spacing (9'x8') is sometimes difficult to maintain on Long Island. This results in unused trellis area, translating to lost income for the grower. The French believe that densely spaced vineyards are a critical component of quality. However, before wide-scale conversion to dense-planting systems, basic questions must be answered, such as the economics of high-density vineyards, effects of high-density on vine growth, fruit quality, plant health, vineyard floor management, spraying, pruning, and training systems. *Project Impact*: High-density plantings have two potential benefits. Yields are reportedly higher in densely spaced plantings. Fruit and wine quality is purported to be improved by closely spacing vines. These are the two most critical issues in any wine growing industry, economically viable yields of high-quality fruit.

Cornell is fully prepared to manage a high-density research vineyard. This project could be located at the Long Island Horticultural Research Lab or in a commercial vineyard on Long Island. A narrow tractor is an integral part of this project because existing vineyard tractors fit only in 8-9' wide rows. The costs associated with a high-density planting are as follows:

One time expenses: $34,100

$25,000	Narrow vineyard tractor, able to fit into 4-5' wide rows
4,000	Sprayer
1,500	Trellis, vineyard installation, one acre
3,600	Grapevines

Yearly Expenses: $14,500

$ 500	Spray materials
8,000	Temp. labor: maintenance, research, harvest, data entry
1,000	Travel Reimbursement (if planted in commercial vineyard)
3,000	Soil, tissue, and fruit testing
2,000	Supplies and materials

3. Grapevine nutrition and fertilization. We have only anecdotal evidence concerning the amounts and types of fertilizers required for vinifera vines on sandy soils. As we endeavor to maintain the quality of our environment and groundwater, we must have detailed guidelines for the use of leachable nutrients. Vine nutrition is a complex issue which can have profound effects on fruit composition. *Project impact*: Determining vine nutritional needs and the optimum timing for nutrient uptake will help growers avoid unnecessary fertilization while maintaining the health and productivity of our vineyards.

Cornell is fully prepared to address this area of research, with the advice of consultants. Cornell currently does not employ a researcher with expertise in this area. Our initial suggestions are to create a tissue analysis data base and to initiate work concerning three major plant nutrients: nitrogen (N), phosphorus (P), and potassium (K).

1. Establish a data base for the varieties Chardonnay, Merlot and Cabernet Sauvignon. Vineyards would provide multiple tissue samples throughout the season, every year for 10 years. This would be used to create a database, useful in tracking trends, comparing tissue nutrient content to weather patterns for the effect of temperature and rainfall, and to evaluate the effectiveness of fertilizer. Samples must be collected by the same 1 or 2 persons in order to maintain experimental integrity and sample uniformity. The costs associated with this project are as follows:

One time expenses: $4,000
$4,000   Computer with hard drive

Yearly Expenses: $14,500
$5,000   Temp. labor: research, data entry
2,000   Travel reimbursement
6,000   Mail/process samples, $200/vineyard block, assuming 30 total blocks
1,000   Consultation fees
500   Supplies and materials

2. Initiate a set of long-term experiments on each of the three major nutrients: nitrogen, phosphorus and potassium. Issues include the effects of fertilizer rate, formulation, organic forms, and foliar vs. ground application on vine and fruit parameters.

One time expenses: none
Computer in experiment above could be used for this project
Otherwise, $4,000 for computer.

Yearly Expenses: $12,500

$7,500	Temp. labor: maintenance, research, harvest, data entry
1,000	Travel reimbursement
2,000	Mail/process samples at Cornell Lab, Ithaca
1,000	Consultation fees
1,000	Supplies and materials

4. Alternative pest controls. We are very eager to increase our use of alternative pest control methods. For example, many regions in Europe have fine tuned the management of spider mites, a common vineyard pest. Their strategies include the use of alternative spray materials such as horticultural oil, intensive scouting and sampling, and encouragement of spider mite predators, other insects which feed on spider mites. This type of work is labor-intensive, long-term, and requires a substantial monetary commitment. Because the blueprint for this work has been established by our European colleagues, the chances for success on Long Island are quite good. *Project impact*: Reducing pesticide use will provide environmental and economic benefits. Pesticides are expensive and growers are eager to adapt less intrusive means of pest control. The use of natural fauna, insects which feed on pest insects, is an attractive strategy from many angles.

This project would involve a Ph.D. entomologist who would research biocontrol for 3 years with the assistance of Alice Wise. This program would evaluate the following:

- Current status of predator populations in Long Island vineyards.
- Identification of spray materials harmful to predators.
- Assessment of the susceptibility of predators collected from upstate vineyards and orchards to pesticides commonly used in Long Island vineyards.
- Release of predators collected from upstate locations in local vineyards, determining their ability to reproduce, survive and control spider mites.

One time expenses: $4,000

$ 4,000	Computer with hard drive

Yearly Expenses: $60,000

$35,000	Postdoctoral research associate salary
13,000	Fringe benefits (36.78%)
3,000	Temporary labor

2,000   Travel and lodging, Geneva personnel
2,000   Vehicle rental
4,000   Computer
1,000   Supplies and materials

5. Rootstock evaluation. Vinifera grapevines are not grown as own-rooted plants. Rather, the variety or scion, the above-ground portion, is grafted onto a rootstock, the below-ground portion. The rootstock imparts resistance to soil-borne pests, vigor control, and hardiness. Rootstocks vary widely in their compatibility with different varieties, adaptation to wet or dry soils, ability to take up nutrients, pest resistance, and so on. This means that a universal rootstock does not exist. A rootstock must, therefore, be matched to the variety, landscape, soil, and desires of the grower. The industry needs a systematic evaluation of rootstocks both in a replicated experimental situation and in the varying conditions of local vineyards. *Project impact*: Choosing a rootstock means making a permanent, irrevocable decision about a planting. The wrong rootstock can profoundly affect yield and fruit composition. Thus, information on proper rootstocks for Long Island could have a number of very positive ramifications, economic and otherwise.

This trial would take place at the Long Island Horticultural Research Lab and in commercial vineyards. At the Lab, a replicated experiment would be initiated, evaluating the effects of 12 or more rootstocks on a single grape variety, Chardonnay.

Expenses, one time, rootstock trial at LIHRL: $10,000
$ 3,000   Plant material
2,000   Grafting
1,000   Cold storage
2,000   Temp. labor: nursery plant, maintain, and fall dig
1,000   Temp. labor: plant and stake permanent vineyard
1,000   Trellis materials and installation

Expenses, yearly, rootstock trial at LIHRL: $8,000
$ 7,000   Temp. labor: maintenance, research, harvest, data entry
1,000   Supplies and materials

The second half of the experiment would evaluate the rootstocks over a range of soil and landscape types. The form of this experiment would depend on the availability of appropriate parcels of land. The costs associated with this trial would be similar, although labor costs would be slightly lower due to in-kind contributions of cooperating grower(s).

Expenses, one time, rootstock trial in vineyards: $8,500

$ 2,000	Plant material
1,000	Grafting
500	Cold storage
2,000	Temp. labor: nursery plant, maintain, and fall dig
2,500	Temp. labor: plant, stake, trellis permanent vineyard (incl. trellis supplies)

Expenses, yearly, rootstock trial in vineyards: $9,000

$ 7,000	Temp. labor: maintenance, research, harvest, data entry
1,000	Travel reimbursement
1,000	Supplies and materials

Proposed Action by the Governor:

THE GOVERNOR SHOULD direct the Department of Agriculture and Markets to fund the above research through the Research and Development Grants Program.

Recommendation #20:

LONG ISLAND WINES SHOULD BE PROMOTED

Background

LONG ISLAND IS a young wine region, the first vineyards planted in the 70's and early 80's. The industry has grown quickly to over 1,500 acres and 17 wineries today. Long Island wines have garnered increasing attention, winning awards and notice at very prestigious wine events. For example, in late October of 1993, the New York Wine Experience was held in New York City. Sponsored by *The Wine Spectator Magazine*, 200 of the world's best wineries were invited to present wines at a grand tasting. In 1993, 5 of the 200 were Long Island wineries, a truly significant feat considering the many fine wineries in Europe, Australia, South America and the U.S.

Promotion of a small wine industry is a challenge. Smaller wineries do not have the financial resources to invest large amounts in promotion. Although local wineries pool their resources through the Long Island Wine Council, promotion of the Long Island wine industry is still done on a relatively small scale. Some of the more successful strategies have involved the production of events, such as Windows on Long Island and the annual Barrel Tasting and BBQ. These events permit the public and the media to meet members of the industry while tasting their wines. They generate press coverage, enthusiasm, contacts and sales for the wineries.

During the July meeting of the East End Economic and Environmental Task Force, Governor Cuomo extended an invitation to the East End wineries to produce a wine-tasting at the Governor's mansion. The goal of this function would be to introduce the full spectrum of Long Island wines to New York restaurants. Restaurants already serving local wines would have an opportunity to try others. Restaurants who have been reluctant to serve local wines could taste the wines and discuss them with wine makers and owners. The potential economic benefits of this tasting could be enormous. In addition, the tasting would generate media interest in both the food and wine of New York.

Coordinating Groups: Governor's staff and the Long Island Wine Council.

Audience: The 100 top New York Restaurateurs, East End legislators and wine press may also be invited.

Suggested dates: November through February, slow times for both wineries and restaurants.

Event format: A 3-4-hour stand-up tasting, held during the evening hours.

Each winery will have a display table from which they pour their wine. Hors d'oeuvres to be served.

Promotion: Press releases, event brochure describing each winery and their wines, event photographer, invitations to wine press, encouragement of local media to cover event.

In-kind from wine industry: Wine, winery staff time to plan, prepare, travel to, participate in, clean-up tasting.

Proposed Action by the Governor:

THE GOVERNOR SHOULD host an East End wine tasting at the Governor's mansion.

Recommendation #21:

THE GRAPE PRICE LAW SHOULD EXEMPT VINIFERA GRAPES

Background

A STATE LAW was passed in 1974 requiring grape buyers to set the price they would pay for grapes by August 15th of each year. The intent of the law was to provide price stability to growers in regions that contained many producers and few buyers. An unanticipated effect of the law is the artificial suppression of grape prices. If conditions change after the August 15th deadline warranting the payment of a higher price for grapes, buyers are prevented from paying growers more for the grapes because of the law. In some areas, therefore, growers are deprived of the maximum value of their crop because they are locked into a lower price.

The Stated Grape Price Law was enacted to provide grape growers with notice of the prices they would receive for their product prior to delivering their grapes to processors. Since grapes are a highly perishable commodity, requiring processors to state the price to be paid in advance allows growers to make crucial harvest and delivery decisions with some assurances of adequate compensation. Unfortunately, the statute has had the unintended effect of depriving growers of a higher price for their grapes after the August 15th deadline, even when processors are willing to pay more. Furthermore, it has prevented processors from responding to market conditions. For example, grape shortages from an early frost normally drive up grape prices. Processors would not be able to match out-of-state prices, thus impairing their ability to obtain sufficient grapes to sustain their operations. Processors who have violated the State Grape Price restrictions have been subject to substantial penalties for paying farmers more than the price stated on August 15th.

The major problem for Long Island wineries concerns the sale of premium Vinifera grapes and Vinifera wines. The problem seems to be that predicting and stating a price on August 15th for the delivery of grapes that may occur as late as mid-October has created production obstacles that hinder grape sales that are advantageous to both the seller and purchaser. This is particularly true for the production of Vinifera wines. The value of Vinifera grapes for wine production, unlike Native American grapes used for juice or bulk wine production, is very dependent on the quality of the fruit, i.e., percentage of rot, sugar content, acid balance, size of berry, location of vineyard. To make premium quality Vinifera wine, the condition of the grape is critical, hence, its quality significantly affects its value. As written, the stated grape price law does not permit fruit quality to be factored into the purchase price. This is because it is impossible for a wine producer or grape grower to predict on August 15th what the quality of the grape will be when it is picked a month or two later. Quality can be affected by too much rain, frost, heat, etc. Further, the processor and small winery must state a single price for all of a Vinifera variety purchased and not base the price on the quality of each shipment of grapes and pay accordingly.

Proposed Action by the Governor:

TO PROMOTE the production of premium wine and to give small wineries some flexibility while, at the same time, ensuring the protection of grape growers and the stability of the grape market, the Governor should propose the following revisions to 250(d) of the Agriculture and Markets Law:

- establish an exemption from the stated price law for all processors that wish to purchase at a price different from their stated price of up to ten tons per grape variety and not to exceed a maximum of twenty tons total, and
- exempt from the law all Vinifera grape varieties such as Chardonnay, Riesling, Cabernet Sauvignon and Merlot.

These changes will not affect the vast majority of the grape market which, in general, sells Native American and French-Hybrid grapes to large processors. However, it will provide flexibility to small- and medium-sized wineries for the production of premium quality Vinifera and French-Hybrid wines. The ultimate goal of such an amendment would be to increase premium wine production and, hence, increase the demand for grapes to the farmer's benefit.

RECREATION/SECOND HOME INDUSTRY

Overview

RECREATION/SECOND HOME INDUSTRY

KEVIN MCDONALD
Vice-President
Group for the South Fork

NANCY NAGLE KELLEY
Associate Director of Development
and Government Relations
Guild Hall of East Hampton

WHEN SETTLERS FIRST arrived on the shores of Long Island's East End over 350 years ago, they encountered pristine beaches, clean waters and bays, fertile farmlands and extensive forests.

The fruits natural to the Island are Mulberries Posimons Grapes, great and small. Plumbs of several sorts and Strawberries of such abundance, that in Spring the fields and woods are died red, which the Country people perceiving instantly arm themselves with bottles of wine, cream and sugar and instead of a coat of male every one takes a Female upon his horse behind him and so rushing violently into the fields never leave them until they have disrobed them of their red colours.

The greatest part of the Island is very full of timber, as oaks white and red, walnut trees, chestnut trees, which yield store of mast for swine, as also maples, cedars, sarsifrage, Beach, Holly, Hazel with many more. The Herbs which the country naturally affords are Purslane, white Orage, Egrimony, violets, penniroyal, Alicompane besides Saxaparilla, very common, with many more, yea, in May you should see the Woods and Fields so curiously bedect with Roses and an innumerable multitude of delightful Flowers not only pleasing to the eye but smell. That you may behold Nature contending with Art and striving to equal if not excel many Gardens in England.

There are divers sorts of singing birds whose chirping notes salute the ears of Travellers with harmonious discord, and in every pond and brook green, silken Frogs who warbling forth their untun'd tunes, strive to bear a part in this musicke.

On the South side of Long Island in winter lie store of Whales and Crampasses of which the Inhabitants begin with small boats to make a grade, catching them to their no small benefit. Also an innumerable multitude of Seals which make an excellent oyle. They lie all winter upon some broken Marshes and Beaches, or bars of sand, and might be easily got were there some skillful men who would undertake it.

A Brief Description of New York, formerly New Netherlands, with the

Places thereunto Adjoining, together with the Manner of its Situation, Fertility of the Soyle &c. Printed in 1670 for John Hancock at the first Shop in Pope's Head Alley in Cornhill at the sign of the Three Bibles.
[This was the first description of New York published in England.]

Fortunately, these priceless resources still exist today, and they form a very strong foundation for the East End's second home/recreation-based economy. Second-home buyers and vacationers view the East End as one of the few unspoiled regions and last vestiges of small town life within driving distance of the New York metropolitan area. The East End has been and continues to be both a recreation destination and an "escape" from the more hectic pace of New York City and western Long Island.

Virtually every study of traveler motivations has shown that, along with rest and recreation, visiting scenic areas and historic sites are among the top reasons why people travel.[2] The hamlets and communities of the East End offer an unparalleled combination of natural and cultural amenities to both the traveler and second-home buyer: world-renowned ocean beaches; bays and harbors rich in finfish and shellfish; scenic farmland vistas and abundant local produce and wines; a real sense of history; quaint villages and specialty shopping; exclusive resorts and affordable inns; diverse outdoor recreational activities; and a strong resale market with respect to real property.

Nowhere is the now familiar adage "our environment is our economy" more prevalent than on the East End of Long Island. The East End's tourism/recreation industry is estimated to be a $1 billion-a-year business. On the East End, over $10 billion has been invested directly in the second-home real estate market. In addition, the extensive services which support these homes form the anchor of the East End economy. The beauty of this $10 billion-plus industry is that, unlike other regions of New York State, which depend on one or two corporate giants for their economic base, this money has been invested by thousands of individuals/shareholders living throughout the area. Thus, it can be viewed as a much more stable investment, not subject to the whims of one or two corporate giants, whose decision to leave an area could wreak long-lasting economic havoc. Yet, the basis of the East End's economy is subject to many variables within our control.

The construction, real estate and insurance industries on the East End are, to a large extent, dependent on the second homeowner who invests in the area only because of its attractive environment.

Over the past two decades, second-home buyers have evolved from strictly summer residents to year-round weekenders to full-time residents.

[2]*Community Appearance and Tourism: What's the Link?*, Edward T. McMahon (*see*, Appendix K).

Many New Yorkers have reversed their commute, using the City for business only 2 to 3 days out of the week, if at all. As a result of this growing trend, once part-time residents are now melding into the local fabric of the East End— placing children in local schools, setting up businesses and cottage industries, involving themselves in local civic and government affairs.

While summer rentals and sales have long been the staple of the local real estate industry, both winter and year-round rentals are increasing in popularity and, as every real estate professional knows, "renters become buyers." Second homeowners are spending considerably more time on the East End and view the area more as a year-round "country" destination than a seasonal summer resort.

The East End is also becoming a more attractive choice as a primary family residence for individuals working "Up-Island" in western Suffolk or eastern Nassau counties. These individuals are being lured east for the same reasons local residents choose to live here and New Yorkers choose to purchase or rent summer homes here: the high-quality environment. Much of the East End's local industry is service-oriented, serving the needs of the second-home and year-round market, as well as the increasing year-round market for tourism.

The East End must continue to be perceived as unique and unspoiled, and maintain, if not enhance, its local character and appeal. Realtors, restaurateurs and resort owners all realize that they must protect the "product" they are trying to sell. The more the East End enhances its unique set of natural and man-made assets, the more the second home/tourist industry will flourish. Conversely, the more suburban it becomes, the less the East End will be seen as an appealing place to purchase a second home or primary residence, to rent for the summer or year-round or just to vacation. As travel writer Arthur Frommer writes, "Tourism simply doesn't go to a place that has lost its soul." Over development, suburbanization, continued loss of open space and scenic vistas, and degradation of natural resources must be avoided.

The East End must develop a strategy for development which meets the daily needs of people and business without compromising the quality of life for the present or that of future generations. On the East End, we recognize that scenic beauty, heritage and environmental quality are good for business. We also recognize that economic growth is necessary and that thriving businesses and industries are necessary to maintain a high quality of life. Here on the East End, economic progress and environmental protection are viewed as part of the same overall goal of maintaining quality of life.

On the East End, sustainable development must strike a balance that *enhances* the agricultural, fishing and second home/recreation industries and *avoids* conflicts which would undermine the area's natural resource-based economy. While a decline in the second-home industry would have far-reaching negative consequences for the East End economy, growth in this industry must be managed in such a way that the East End's special character is not compromised or lost forever. The sensitivity of the high environmental quality which is the very foundation of the East End's economy is also what directs growth options for the region.

The East End is at a critical crossroads when it comes to preserving its economic and environmental future. The following pages offer a number of proposed actions for the Governor to take to help insure a bright future for the East End.

NATURAL RESOURCES

Recommendation #22:

THE LAND ACQUISITION PARTNERSHIP BETWEEN THE STATE AND LOCAL GOVERNMENTS SHOULD BE EXPANDED

Background

THE CONTINUED STATE, County and local Open Space acquisition programs are essential to the economic and environmental future of the East End.

There are 8,987 areas of State-owned land on the East End (*see*, Appendix Q). The 1992 New York State Open Space Plan specifically identifies more of the East End's landscapes and natural resources as needing protection.

Suffolk County has already invested $200 million in watershed protection and $65 million in farmland preservation. Local towns have invested more than $40 million in local land acquisition initiatives in the last 15 years. They have done so with broad voter support because of the public understanding that protection of a high-quality environment, outstanding recreational opportunities, rural character and scenic beauty across the East End make this region special and unlike any other in the New York metropolitan area. If the East End loses its unique sense of place, the industries which hinge upon the above attributes would be imperiled.

According to Edward T. McMahon, Senior Associate at the Conservation Fund and former President of Scenic America

> "Tourism involves much more than marketing. It also involves making destinations more appealing. This means conserving and enhancing a destination's natural tourism assets. It is, after all, the heritage, culture and natural beauty of a community or region that attracts tourism." (*See*, Appendix K.)

The East End of Long Island contains the highest concentrations of rare and endangered plants and animals in New York State.[3] Although the five eastern towns and villages have implemented some of the most progressive and innovative planning techniques on the country,[4] some parcels require full

---

[3] New York State Natural Heritage Program.

[4] These towns have a variety of programs including: purchase of development rights; transfer of development rights; mandatory cluster ordinances; wetlands setback ordinances; beach, dune and bluff protection ordinances; flood hazard regulations; coastal hazard regulations; historic districts; special groundwater protection regulations; harbor protection regulations (pending); tree protection ordinances; critical environmental area designations pursuant to SEQRA, zoning; subdivision and site plan ordinances; etc.

acquisition to preserve these sensitive features. In other words, **any** development of these parcels would cause irreparable harm to the features requiring protection.

"Greenways" are corridors of protected open space. No other conservation initiative provides so many ecological, economic and quality of life benefits to the communities that create them. Greenways not only protect environmentally important lands, they also link people with the natural world and outdoor recreational opportunities.[5] Greenways and open space enhance property values, support local recreation-based businesses,[6] enhance tourism, encourage relocation, and reduce public cost of unwise development.[7]

Proposed Action by the Governor:
A. Large Parcels

PRIORITY PARCELS listed below are all within the Peconic Pinelands Maritime Reserve cited in the State's 1992 Open Space Plan. We request that the Governor working with the Commissioner of the Department of Environmental Conservation and the Office of Parks, Recreation and Historic Preservation develop a 5-year protection plan to accomplish the preservation of the priority parcels. The plan would include an assessment of the degree of threat to each parcel and identify source of funds for each parcel including partnerships with town, county and federal government and non-profit conservation organizations.

East Hampton Town

Culloden—Named after the *H.M.S. Culloden*, which sank off Montauk, this 275-acre parcel has outstanding views of Block Island Sound, wetlands, and the potential for an underwater park.

The Sanctuary—393 acres owned by ICR/Montauk. Resources values include: endangered species, wetlands, trails; logical addition to State park land.

Shadmoor—98 acres owned by Peter Schub and Robert Bear, Montauk, Resource values include: ocean access (swimming, surfing, fishing), trails, scenic views, federally endangered species, wetlands, historic importance.

---

[5]The American Greenway Program—The Conservation Fund.

[6]Economic Impacts of Protecting Rivers, Trails and Greenway Corridors, National Park Service, 1990. American Greenways Program.

[7]More and more studies are showing that conserving open land and choosing carefully those areas that should be developed is not contrary to economic health but essential to it. Holly Thomas, Senior Planner, Dutchess County Planning Department. *See*, Appendix L.

Southampton Town

Cow Neck—980 acres owned by Peter Salm, North Sea. Resource values include: bay access (swimming, boating, fishing), wetlands, wildlife concentrations, endangered species, consolidation of park land (adjacent to federal, town and Nature Conservancy lands), scenic views.

Bridgehampton Racetrack—518 acres owned by Robert M. Rubin. Resource values include: possible conversion of racetrack area to public golf course, water recharge.

South Shore National Seashore Extension—Approximately 300 acres/various owners. Resource values include: ocean access (swimming), bay access (boating, shellfishing/fishing), endangered species, wildlife concentrations, scenic views, storm protection.

Riverhead Town

Jamesport—517 acres owned by LILCO. Resource values include: Long Island Sound access (swimming, boating, fishing), trails, historic and scenic views, farmland, buffer to Hallockville Farm Museum.

Riverhead Hamlet—Approximately 65 acres comprised of small parcels along the south side of New York State Route 25, between Nugent Drive (a/k/a Center Drive) and Forge Road. Regulated pursuant to Wild, Scenic and Recreational Rivers designation. Resource values include: Peconic River access (boating, fishing), scenic vistas, wildlife habitats, enhancement of downtown area.

Olin Warner, Peconic River—30 Acres—800 feet of Peconic Lake shorefront, provides public access for freshwater fishing, canoeing, and nature observance.

Southold Town

Robins Island—445 acres owned by Southold Development Corp. Resource values include: bay access (swimming, boating, fishing), endangered species, historic and scenic views, trails, wetlands, environmental education.

Orient Point Additions—Approximately 300 acres/numerous owners. Resource values include: addition to State and county park land, wetlands, endangered species, farmland, bay access (boating, swimming, fishing), historic and scenic views.

Dam Pond—114 acres. Resource values include: Long Island Sound access (swimming, boating, fishing), ponds/wetlands, wildlife concentrations, scenic views.

Fort Corchaug—106 acres. Indian fort location.

Shelter Island

Groundwater recharge lands. Approximately 500+ acres. Resource values include: groundwater recharge, trails, wetlands/ponds. Such parcels will be further identified pursuant to the Town's anticipated adoption of its first comprehensive plan.

Southampton/East Hampton Towns Combined

South Fork Morainal Woodlands (Paumanok Path connection)—Southampton/East Hampton Towns. Approximately 4,000 acres/numerous owners. Last concentrations of large blocks of land on the South Fork. Resource values include: groundwater recharge, trails, kettle holes ponds, forest preservation, and wildlife concentrations. This section includes:

Central Pine Barrens

Southampton/Riverhead/Brookhaven Towns. Approximately 10,000 acres. Resource values include: water recharge, trails, endangered species, wildlife concentrations, wetlands/ponds, environmental education.

B. Small Parcels

IN ADDITION TO the large parcels identified for acquisition, there are numerous vacant parcels, five acres or less in size, created prior to the adoption of zoning which are eligible for building permits without any subdivision. Some of these parcels are too constrained to construct a single-family residence, contain 100% wetlands, do not meet the State Tidal or Freshwater Wetland Regulations and/or do not meet the State and County Sanitary Code Regulations for construction. Yet, State DEC and Health Department Agencies often issues a permit to build on such a lot because a denial would amount to a taking. Rather than grant state permits to lots which should not be built upon, we recommend that the Governor make State funds available through the Environmental Protection Act and other available sources to provide for purchase of such properties.[8]

---

[8]This recommendation compliments Recommendation #24 (Enforcement of Tidal and Freshwater Wetland Laws Should be Delegated to Towns).

Recommendation #23:

EXISTING REGULATORY ENVIRONMENTAL OBJECTIVES SHOULD BE SUPPLEMENTED WITH INCENTIVES

Background

CURRENTLY, most environmental and health-related public policy objectives are accomplished with regulatory (command and control) techniques. There are two shortcomings to this approach: 1) this regulatory approach has limits to its reach and 2) it is not always successful in reaching its desired goal.[9] The negative reinforcement techniques of traditional regulatory policy also require substantial commitments of funds and staff to enforce the "forced" restrictions they impose.

For instance, today, the existing wetland regulatory programs are unable to affect development sites which were built before the effective date of the statute. Therefore, pre-existing conditions like septic systems close to water bodies, lawns and the fertilizers and pesticides which run down to the water's edge are contributing to the degradation of water quality. Currently, there is little being done to abate this.

Under the current regulatory framework, septic systems are only upgraded by requiring the applicant to undertake such action as a condition of approval of a permit, if a permit is being sought at all. This presents a few problems. One, if the property owner is not making improvements to the property, the pre-existing conditions continue; and, second, requirements of such conditions are sometimes not complied with.

If it is desirable to restore wetland buffers, upgrade septic systems, and replace leaking underground home heating oil fuel tanks, then these objectives should be achieved directly, rather than indirectly. If the goal is to maximize environmental compliance, the tools available to accomplish this should be expanded, and should include positive reinforcement and incentive techniques. For example, when New York State offered energy tax credits, the obvious incentive resulted in many New York State residents instituting energy conservation measures.

---

[9]Osborne & Graber, Reinventing Government.

Proposed Action by the Governor:

1) Real property Tax Abatements. The Governor should introduce legislation under §§487(a) and 487(b) of the Real Property Tax Law to enable towns to grant real property tax abatements[10] to accomplish enhanced environmental compliance for qualified environmental projects, such as: replacement of underground gasoline and home heating oil tanks, upgrading of septic systems, commercial/residential stormwater water abatement projects and restoration of wetland buffers.

Need for Legislation. The proposed legislation would protect surface waters, wetlands, and groundwater. Scientific evidence shows that wetlands and surface waters are degraded where stormwater run-off, septic system effluent, or fuel oil enters ecosystems. The introduction of these pollutants can be minimized by preventing stormwater from entering surface waters either by the use of structural measures, such as recharge basins, or the restoration of wetland buffers, which absorb pollutants. The environment can also be protected by upgrading old septic systems which are working improperly and replacing leaking fuel oil tanks. Tax incentives could encourage these measures.

Existing Legislation. Real Property Tax Law ("RPTL") 300 requires that all real property in the state be taxed unless exempt from state law. While state law lists numerous exemptions to promote certain public policy objectives, the items listed above are not exempted. Municipal Home Rule Law §1(d)(3) prohibits towns from superseding a "state statute relating to…(2) creation or alteration of areas of taxation." Therefore, specific state enabling legislation is necessary to enable towns to give tax relief to those who undertake these projects. RPTL presently attempts to encourage residents to undertake conservation measures. For example, RPTL §487 gives an exemption from taxation for certain solar or wind energy systems and §487-a grants exemptions for conservation improvements, such as insulation and energy conservation measures to certain residential premises. The proposed legislation would be consistent with same.

Specific Amendments. Section 487-a of the RPTL should be amended to include the conservation measures cited above. In the alternative, a new §487-

---

[10]This is modeled after a state law which exempts capital improvements to real property in the first year and then phases in the increase in assessment over the next seven years. This bill permits localities to grant an eight-year property-tax exemption for home improvements; permits counties and school districts to opt out of the exemption granted by a city, town or village; deems the exemption to be 100% of increased assessed value in the first year, to decrease by 12.5% annually in each of the next seven years; limits the value of the improvement eligible for the exemption to $80,000, but allows the locality to lower the limit to $5,000; establishes eligibility criteria and administrative procedures; and does not apply to New York City.

b could be added entitled, "Exemption from taxation of improvements that aid environmental protection." Listed under this section would be septic system upgrade, fuel oil tank replacement, or drainage improvements. A separate section could be added numbered 487-c to give a tax break to those who restore wetland buffers or stop stormwater from entering surface waters by nonstructural means.

It is envisioned any town willing to implement this tax abatement would need to do so pursuant to a locally adopted plan outlining the condition needing remediation, the extent of the problem, the incentive to the recipient and the impact on the tax base. It is envisioned that towns would be able to craft programs to be limited and targeted to specific needs, with sunset provisions and other limits so as to not create unpredictable and unforeseen administrative complications and unnecessary negative fiscal impacts on the tax base.

2) Environmental Improvement Income Tax Deduction. The Governor should introduce legislation under Article 22 of the Tax Law to provide for a tax deduction under New York State income tax laws to enable interest deductions for certain qualified environmental projects (similar to those mentioned above in (1) and permit lending institutions to be exempted from earned income for the same types of loans. This could result in more favorable financial yields to encourage the environmental policy objective sought.

A. *Existing Legislation.* The tax law is presently designed to promote certain public policy objectives by granting income tax relief to those who undertake measures beneficial to society as a whole. For example, special treatment is granted at §606 and §612 of the Tax Law for solar and wind energy systems in the form of a tax credit.

Specific Amendments. Tax Law §§601 to 699 should be amended appropriately to provide the necessary tax relief.

B. *Existing Legislation.* Currently, interest income earned by lending institutions is factored in to compute net income and, thus, is taxable in New York State. Lending institutions that receive interest income from municipalities are exempt from State tax which provides for lower municipal interest rates. This recommendation envisions banks developing environmental improvement loan portfolios with exemptions similar to those afforded municipalities whose interest payments are exempt from State taxation. The effect of this recommendation would enable businesses and residents to make environmental improvements to their property at less than prevailing market interest rates.

Specific Amendments. The Tax Law should be amended appropriately to incorporate this provision.

3) Improvement Districts. The Governor should introduce legislation under §190 of the Town Law modeled after the New York State Water Quality Improvement District Law passed in 1984. This law would work as follows: Classes of property needing remediation in each of the towns would be identified and would then be eligible to have certain improvements made (drainage, wetland buffer restoration, upgrading septic systems, replacement of underground home heating oil tanks, etc.). Each town would create a new taxing district to pay for the improvements, and the properties within the district would receive the benefit of municipal finance rates, favorable terms to pay certain improvements or municipal requests for proposals to undertake certain of the tasks identified.

Existing Legislation. Town Law §190 presently enables municipalities to establish improvement districts, including sewer, drainage, water, water quality treatment, water supply, and harbor improvement districts, among others, and to provide improvements or services wholly at the expense of the district. Town law §198 lists the powers of Town Boards with respect to these districts.

Specific Amendments. Town Law §190 should be amended to establish a number of new districts, including town-wide septic system districts and town-wide fuel oil tank districts, which would promote the goals already discussed. If town-wide districts are not possible, the boundaries of these new districts could be within deep-flow water recharge areas and within 500 feet of any wetland or water body. These two areas are particularly sensitive to the negative impacts of septic systems and fuel oil.

Instead of establishing new improvement districts, it may be possible to amend existing districts to permit these ends. For example, Town Law §190-e, Wastewater Disposal Districts, makes reference to "on-site wastewater disposal systems." However, it is unclear whether or not this pertains to private septic systems or simply to collection districts for the purpose of transporting sewage to sewage treatment plans. This section could be amended or clarified in a manner that includes private on-site septic system improvements. Town Law §198(2) addresses the subject of drainage districts. Rather than adding a new district with respect to stormwater abatement, this section could be amended.

In addition, a wetlands buffer restoration district could be established. Moneys from this district could be utilized to re-establish wetland buffers and to purchase wetland areas.

Town Law §198 would also have to be amended to reflect the powers of town boards with respect to the new amended districts.

4) Allow Citizens to Initiate Legislation that Protects the

Environment. The Governor should introduce legislation which enables citizens to put the environmental protection measures discussed above to a public vote which will result in money to pay for these measures.

Existing Legislation. Town §81 presently allows citizens to place a number of issues on the ballot without Town Board approval, i.e., to initiate legislation. Town Law §81(g), however, is vague with respect to the measures suggested above. It provides "The town board may upon its own motion and shall upon a petition,…cause to be submitted at a special or biennial town election, a proposition:…1) in any town:…g) To dredge, bulkhead, dock and otherwise improve navigable, or other waterways, within the town…". Whether or not such improvements could include septic tank upgrade, fuel oil tank replacement, or wetland buffer restoration and the like is unclear.

Specific Amendment. Town Law §81(g) should be clarified to include these measures or an additional section should be added.

Recommendation #24:

ENFORCEMENT OF TIDAL AND FRESHWATER WETLAND LAWS SHOULD BE DELEGATED TO TOWNS AND VILLAGES

Background

THE NEW YORK STATE Tidal Wetlands Act is administered by the Department of Environmental Conservation and regulates most activities within 300 feet of any tidal wetland. This law was passed in 1973 when most local governments were seen as unable to adequately protect the resource. Today, many municipalities have adopted local tidal wetland laws which are more protective than the State law.[11]

The Freshwater Wetlands Act (FWWA) provides for local regulation of certain types of Freshwater Wetlands.[12] However, the provision technically requires local municipalities to adopt the State's program rather than developing their own.

Due to the extensive development of the New York Metropolitan area, the substantial bulk of Fresh and Tidal Wetlands of high quality are found on the East End of Long Island. The vast majority of all wetland permits reviewed and issued by New York are for the East End of Long Island. This reflects population, development pressure and acreage of wetlands found on the East End.

Proposed Action by the Governor:

THE GOVERNOR SHOULD proposed a program bill to amend Article 25 of the Environmental Conservation Law (Tidal Wetlands Act) and Article 24 of the Environmental Conservation Law (Freshwater Wetlands Act) to enable delegation of these laws in their entirety to qualifying local governments. Local governments should qualify upon demonstrating that the local law is

---

[11]Currently, DEC Tidal Wetland Regulations require 75-foot setbacks for structures and 100-foot setbacks for septic systems.

[12]The DEC Freshwater Wetlands regulations do not specify wetland setbacks, per se. DEC regional policy is flexible regarding setbacks and often results in 50-foot structural setbacks and 100-foot septic system setbacks. The State FWW Act does not allow DEC to delegate to local government permit authority over Class I wetlands, and wetlands designated as "Local and unusual importance." This provision still requires the applicant to seek permits from local government and the state.

able to accomplish the purpose of the state statute and that the local government has the demonstrated technical and administrative competence to implement the law.[13] The DEC could retain audit powers to review local government decisions and revoke the local implementation if the purpose of the state laws are not upheld by local government.

---

[13]This recommendation envisions the continuance of the agricultural exemption.

Overview

TRANSPORTATION

THE CONGESTED ROADWAYS of the South and North Forks during the peak summer season are legendary and often detract from the other outstanding attributes of the East End. In the past, the principal solution considered had been the construction of a new two- or four-lane highway. The most recent State Department of Transportation study of the Montauk Highway corridor prepared by Vollmer Associates essentially concluded that such a new highway would not resolve the region's traffic problems and would have significant adverse effects on the community.[14]

Demand for Travel and the Price of Travel

"In choosing a particular mode of travel—and in deciding whether to make a trip at all—the traveler compares the price of available alternatives. This price has several major components:
- price in money
- price in travel time
- price in access time and effort
- price in discomfort and disamenity.

A high price of travel—measured by the sum of these components—will tend to suppress travel demand. Reducing the price of travel by any particular mode—such as reducing travel time by offering higher speed—will have a threefold effect: it will induce new travel, which would not have been considered worthwhile at the previous high price to the user; it will divert some travel from competing modes, whose comparative position will no longer be as attractive as it was before; and it will tend in the long run to relocate travel destinations (residences and nonresidential facilities) in accordance with the new pattern of easier access, thus further reinforcing the demand for the preferred mode." *Public Transportation and Land Use Policy*, Pushkarev & Zupan, 1977.

With the passage of the Federal Intermodel Surface Transportation Act (ISTEA) of 1991, one of the country's most important transportation initia-

---

[14]While implementation of certain of the alternatives investigated would help to alleviate travel conditions, they would not be sufficient nor would they provide satisfactory traffic benefits in relation to their impacts to warrant such an enormous investment. For example, the alternative to reconstructing Montauk Highway into four lanes was the only alternative (highway or transit) which would provide the corridor with a reasonable level of service. Unfortunately, it also would have severe adverse social and environmental impacts on the surrounding community and would be the most expensive alternative to construct.

tives, new opportunities for relief may be provided to the East End's transportation problems. Under ISTEA, Congress has for the first time recognized that alternatives to automobiles as a principal means of moving people and minimizing congestion should be a major focus of future transportation initiatives. ISTEA seeks to fully encourage all levels of transportation based on the specific needs of an area.

Recommendation #25:

A PARK AND RAIL FOR RESIDENTS AND VISITORS TO THE EAST END AND OTHER TRANSPORTATION IMPROVEMENTS SHOULD BE CONSTRUCTED

Background

South Fork

THE PROPOSAL[15] involves establishing new LIRR stations adjacent to Westhampton Airport, Shinnecock Hills near the College, between the railroad and East Hampton Airport and to increase parking space at Montauk. These stations would be served by special "Park and Rail" trains on Friday and Saturday eastbound, and Sunday and Monday westbound from mid-May to early October. The existing stations would still be used by regular passengers.

The idea would be to encourage city residents who summer on the South Fork to bring their cars out at the start of the season, leave them out here, then return them to the city when they leave for the winter. Each of these stops would have fenced parking lots guarded around the clock so that the users would be assured that their automobiles will not be vandalized or stolen. On Friday evenings, a qualified mechanic would be on-hand in case any customer has car trouble. The service would be incredibly fast, clear, efficient and relaxing.

Currently, it can take four hours to drive from the west side of Manhattan to Montauk on a Friday in July. The train would make it in just two-and-a-half refreshing hours, stopping only at the special stations. Once off the train, passengers would get in their waiting cars, then drive out along Montauk Highway against the flow of traffic, thereby greatly alleviating the jams we have come to know all too well. People who live from Amagansett east would use the Montauk facility; those who reside in Bridgehampton and Southampton would get off the train at East Hampton airport; those in Hampton Bays and Quogue would disembark at Shinnecock Hills, and those in the Westhampton to Moriches area would use the Westhampton stop.

There would be additional inducements to encourage the success of this service. The railroad would sell "reserve" commuter tickets, ranging from a minimum of the ten-week high summer season to five months during the long

---

[15]Ron Zeil, the originator of this concept, is a regular contributor to *The East Ender*. He's widely known as a railroad authority who has written some 14 books on the subject of railroading.

season (eventually year-round, if the public reaction to the service warrants) at about 65% of the cost of the equivalent one-way fares, just as present commuter tickets are sold. There would be parlor cars for those wishing to enjoy additional amenities, such as plush seats, beverage and snack service and porters.

There would, of course, be a charge for the use of the parking facilities, to cover the construction and maintenance costs. Costs would range from about $250 for the ten-week peak season to $400 for twenty weeks. Other details would have to be worked out and some minor additional highway improvement may be required to allow access to Sag Harbor and East Hampton without having to go near the Montauk Highway.

This program would ease the traffic not only on Route 27 in the Hamptons, but the Long Island Expressway and Sunrise Highway further west as well. Summer residents and guests would arrive happy and refreshed, ready to go out and spend money, rather than frustrated and nursing a migraine headache. If the population grows on the North Fork, a similar service could be inaugurated along the LIRR mainline, with possible stops at Aquebogue, Peconic and between Southold and Greenport. The service would also provide more jobs: railroad personnel, parking lot guards and others.

North Fork

The North Fork faces a transportation scenario comparable to that of the South Fork. The rail system is badly deteriorated and serves only a small fraction of the traveling public. There are two parallel east/west roads for much of the North Fork and only one for the Eastern portion. The experience on the South Fork is highly relevant to the North Fork: where car traffic often overwhelms road capacity in Southampton and parts of East Hampton Towns, there is still time to make the necessary changes on the North Fork and where community opposition precludes many possible solutions on the South Fork, there is still an opportunity to make the necessary improvements on the North Fork. In short, Southold Town needs preventive measures to develop its business- and tourist-related opportunities before its limited transport network is unable to serve people efficiently—a day that is virtually upon us.

The growth in traffic to and from the Orient Ferry is an example of how rapidly the traffic problem has grown. Those ferries load and unload every hour during the summer and fall with over 300 cars on the larger boats. The majority of this traffic travels through the North Fork and on, leaving residents sometimes even unable to get onto Route 25 from their driveways.

The Town of Southold is attempting to address these problems. Its Stewardship Task Force has recommended the improvement of rail service including the addition of rail shuttle service between North Fork hamlets along with the development of alternate forms of transportation within Town for tourists such as mini-buses and vans. In response to these recommendations, the Town is applying for ISTEA funding to help design and construct an interactive network of bicycle and pedestrian trails with State Route 25, our primary east-west link from Riverhead to the Orient Ferry.

Proposed Action by the Governor:

THE GOVERNOR SHOULD request the State Department of Transportation and the Metropolitan Transportation Authority, including the Long Island Railroad, to implement improvements to the East End transportation system as outlined herein. This should be done in cooperation with the Supervisors and Mayors of the affected Towns and Villages.

Further, the Governor should instruct the State Department of Transportation to commission a survey of projected transportation needs on the North Fork and propose ways of dealing with those needs, keeping in view recent experience from the South Fork. The survey should deal primarily with car traffic but should also recognize and integrate growing roles for rail transportation and mini-buses and other transport systems, such as the proposed bike trails (*see*, Recommendation #27). The purpose of this survey should be to prepare an action plan to keep the North Fork transportation system a viable means to serve the traveling public while preserving the environmental amenities which both visitors and residents value so highly.

Recommendation #26:

A SHUTTLE RAIL SERVICE TO RUN BETWEEN VILLAGES SHOULD BE IMPLEMENTED

Background

THIS PROPOSAL USES the existing LIRR tracks as a shuttle (or series of shuttles) to run between hamlets when there are no commuter trains running. For instance, the shuttle would run between Montauk and East Hampton, East Hampton to Southampton and Southampton to Westhampton with local stops in-between, with a similar structure on the North Fork. Individuals would travel in a two-car nostalgic trolley-type car, which would be both fun for touring riders and functional for people more interested in moving from one place to another. There are some very pleasant scenic aspects of a train shuttle route on both forks and significant savings in travel time. Such a concept would incorporate bike racks on shuttles.

Peak Summer Travel Days; Time comparisons are as follows:

	By Train[16] (Minutes)	By Car[17] (Minutes)
Hampton Bays to Southampton Village	14	30
Hampton Bays to Bridgehampton	21	60
Hampton Bays to East Hampton	30	85
Hampton Bays to Montauk	56	120

The shuttle concept would most likely require re-routing some buses to help move people from train and shuttle stations to other locations, and a bus shuttle from train stations to hamlets.

Proposed Action by the Governor:

THE GOVERNOR SHOULD request the State Department of Transportation and the Metropolitan Transportation Authority, including the Long Island Railroad, to implement improvements to the East End transportation system as outlined above. This should be done in consultation with the Supervisors and Mayors of the affected Towns and Villages.

---

[16] 1993 Saturday train schedule, Long Island Railroad.
[17] Best estimates.

Recommendation #27:

A NETWORK OF BIKE PATHS SHOULD BE CREATED

Background

BICYCLE RIDING HAS BEEN increasing in popularity, both as a recreational activity and as an alternative form of transportation. However, the narrow road shoulders and congested roadway characteristics on the East End make hazardous bicycle riding conditions. On the South Fork, the active railroad lines and rights-of-way connect every major hamlet and population center. Group for the South Fork and the Town of East Hampton are developing a plan to provide bike paths adjacent to the LIRR corridor and thereby provide a safe, scenic alternative transportation and recreation route. The Town intends to submit an ISTEA grant application to survey, design, acquire rights-of-way, when necessary, and construct a portion of this bikeway. On the North Fork, the bike paths could be created on County Road 48.

The recreational benefits of added bike and trail facilities and season-extending opportunities are very promising.[18] The National Park Service is currently undertaking a Technical Assistance Grant to help develop the Paumanok Path, a hiking trail from Rocky Point in Brookhaven to Montauk. The development of trails and bike paths would also have the spin-off effect of creating the need for additional bike rental operations and other services.

Proposed Action by the Governor:

THE GOVERNOR SHOULD direct MTA and the Long Island Railroad officials to assist in the realization of this plan and he should direct the DOT to fund bikeways through ISTEA transportation enhancement funds.

---

[18]The Town of East Hampton trail maps for Montauk, Northwest Woods and Napeague are very popular and coveted. Regarding the impact of trails and bikeways on property values, property near but not immediately adjacent to Seattle's Burke Gilman trail is significantly easier to sell and, according to real estate agents, sells for an average of 6% more as a result of its proximimty to the trails.

Overview

MARINE INDUSTRY

PETER NEEDHAM
Marine Operator

THE EAST END'S MARINE INDUSTRY is a major component of the area's economy. This industry, which includes marinas, boatyards, boat dealers, marine supply stores and other related enterprises, often goes unrecognized because it is composed of a large number of individual businesses that are usually relatively small.

While the individual businesses may be small, the recreational and economic benefits the marine industry provides to the East End are substantial. A large part of the East End's tourist industry is dependent on the recreational boating activity that these businesses attract and support. A recent study done in conjunction with the U.S. EPA's Long Island Sound Study found that recreational boating was the single most important economic activity associated with use of the Sound (Altobello 1992). In 1990, the annual value of boating on the Sound was estimated to be $3.3 billion compared to $1 billion for sport fishing, $842 million for swimming and $148 million for commercial fishing. Boating accounted for over 60 percent of the total economic value of the Sound, estimated at $5.5 billion annually.

Based on figures obtained from a recent New York Sea Grant industry survey, the 122 commercial marina facilities on the East End of Long Island alone generate an estimated $115,785,800 in gross revenues from dockage, boat sales, storage, repairs and services and sales. These facilities employed over 1,300 people with a payroll of over $35,000,000 and paid over $13,200,000 in taxes in 1992. Applying a multiplier of 2.2, which has been found to be representative for the boating industry in the Northeast, marinas generate over $250 million in direct and indirect expenditures on the East End of Long Island. These figures do not reflect expenditures at other boating related businesses such as marine electronic firms, inland sales and repair shops, canvas and sail makers, etc.

More importantly, recreational boating stimulates economic activity outside the marina. Studies here and elsewhere have shown that for every dollar boaters spend in a marina, they spend one to two dollars in the surrounding community on trip-related expenses, such as food, gas, and lodging.

Recreational boating facilities generate another $100 to $200 million in direct expenditures for area businesses such as groceries, restaurants, delicatessens, gas stations and motels patronized by the boater.

Commercial marine facilities, such as marinas, provide access to coastal waters to millions of New York residents who cannot afford waterfront property. According to the State Office of Parks and Recreation, over 5.5 million New Yorkers participate in boating annually. Boating is a cornerstone of the East End's tourist industry and one of the primary reasons this area is considered a premier resort destination. Marine businesses provide the access and services necessary to support this activity at no cost to the government.

Although marinas serve as the gateway to the water for millions of New York residents, they occupy a very small part of the environmentally sensitive shoreline area. According to the study prepared by the Suffolk County Brown Tide Comprehensive Assessment and Management Plan, less than 0.4 percent of the land in the Peconic's drainage basin is used for marine commercial activity. The average Long Island marina only covers 2.6 acres but provides slips (and water access) for 83 families or individuals. Not only is the percentage of land used small compared to industrial, residential and agricultural shoreline uses, but boating activity is highly seasonal and usually limited to a short period of time, minimizing some of the environmental impacts associated with human uses of our coastal resources.

Unfortunately, the marine industry of the East End is facing a number of problems that are limiting its ability to provide public access to the coast and contribute to the regional economy. In some cases, these problems threaten the existence of the industry itself. This industry typically operates at a very low profit margin, usually less than 5%, and is very sensitive to changes in the general economy. Nationwide, the recession has resulted in a 37% decrease in marine retail sales between 1987 and 1992, according to the National Marine Manufacturers Association. The East End marine industry has seen similar losses which jeopardize the viability of many businesses.

Because they must be located on the waterfront, marine businesses must meet some of the strictest environmental standards in their operations. Impending point and non-point source pollution regulations being developed at the state and federal level will require many of these enterprises to undertake costly modifications to bring their facilities into compliance. Implementation of proposed environmental requirements could drive smaller, less-profitable enterprises out of business.

When improvements can be made, marine facilities' owners are often stymied by a complex permitting process for coastal work that requires approvals of a myriad of local, state and federal agencies that often have conflicting mandates and little or no coordination. Obtaining the State permits needed to improve or expand a facility, especially Tidal Wetlands permits, can take two to five years. In many cases, the cost and time associated with the permit process alone prevents operators from making needed repairs and improvements.

The following recommendations address some of the most pressing problems facing the East End's marine industry and offer some suggestions that will enhance the viability of these businesses, improve the interaction between the business and regulatory communities and, most importantly, stimulate the economy while protecting the area's natural resources.

Recommendation #28:

PROGRAMS TO RETAIN MARINA FACILITIES ON THE EAST END SHOULD BE CREATED

Background

THE MARINAS ARE one of the few water-dependent uses found on the East End and are part of East End's maritime heritage. The recently released draft report prepared by the New York State Department of State entitled "Long Island Sound Coastal Management Program" states that:

> "Marinas help support leisure activities associated with and dependent upon coastal resources. In a region where public access opportunities are inadequate, marinas provide a type of access to coastal waters and areas otherwise inaccessible to the public."

The East End has seen explosive residential development of the shoreline. According to the BTCAMP study, less than 0.4 percent of the land in the Peconic drainage basin is used for marine commercial activity. While the land usage is small compared to residentially developed shoreline, the typical marina provides access for an average of 83 families per facility. Those not fortunate enough to afford waterfront property turn to recreational boating as a way of gaining access to and enjoying the East End's natural resources.

Unfortunately, marinas face increasing pressure to convert their limited waterfront areas to non-water-dependent uses such as restaurants or residential development including condominiums. According to the "North Atlantic Water Dependent Use Study" done by the Maine Marine Law Institute for the New England/New York Coastal Task Force:

> "...regardless of size and profitability of marinas, none is immune to the lure of higher profits from conversion to non-water-dependent uses."

A number of states have recognized the importance of preserving maritime industries and have implemented programs intended to retain these businesses on the waterfront. In Massachusetts, Coastal Zone Management was directed in 1987 to expend two million dollars on purchasing development rights from boatyards to thwart the increasing conversion of waterfront businesses to other non-water-dependent-use purposes. Florida has lowered fees

Recreation/Second Home Industry

for water-dependent businesses and is examining several forms of "blue belting" legislation which provide economic incentives to help marina and boat yard owners resist the strong economic pressure to sell their properties to others who would convert it to non-marine uses.

While New York State has striven to enact programs aimed at preserving farmland, there has been little effort or recognition given to the retention of marinas. The Governor's Task Force on Coastal Resources found:

> "Water-dependent businesses contend with many of the same land use and tax issues that agricultural uses face."[19]

Like farms, in many instances, land values for water-dependent businesses have been reassessed to reflect the highest-and-best-use despite the current use as a working waterfront business. Estate tax valuation techniques employed by federal and state officials seek to value property for its highest-and-best use, typically residential condominiums, even though zoning regulations would not allow this conversion.

Along with these tax disincentives, strict environmental scrutiny by local, state and federal regulators has also contributed to the conversion of marinas to non-water-dependent uses or to the decision of the business to leave the area. These constraints limit the growth potential necessary for economic viability.

According to figures obtained from a recent New York Sea Grant industry survey, on average, the expenses associated with operating a commercial facility on the East End in 1992 exceeded gross revenues. This trend has seen the demise of many small marinas which were typically family owned and operated, their interest being sold to corporate entities or foreclosed upon by mortgage institutions.

Proposed Action by the Governor:

1. The Governor should call for legislation to establish a New York State Marina "Right to the Waterfront" Preservation Program.

2. The Governor should call for legislation to offer protection from the practice of taxing marine facilities at highest-and-best use. In as much as this part deals with exceptions or abatements, we recommend the following addition to New York State Real Property Tax Law, Title 4, (new) §583:

---

[19]*Now and for the Future: A Vision for New York's Coast.*

§583 Value of lands supporting private or commercial water-dependent activities. Notwithstanding any other provision of law, real property owned or leased for water-dependent activities, being a corporation, d/b/a, or individual, shall be assessed for the purposes of this chapter on those structures that shall be defined as those used:

1. *For the purpose of berthing and mooring of recreational vessels, and the storage thereof, or a boatyard, marine service facility, charter or sports fishing station, bait and fuel operations, marine towing, or*

2. *For any other non-residential purpose (including motel or condominium use) that requires the use of waterfront lands in order to function or provide marine services, and*

3. *Within a marine district as defined by Coastal Zone Management Local Waterfront Revitalization Program, or within a state approved Harbor Management Plan, or,*

4. *On lands under lease from the State of New York, or the Thruway Authority, for non-residential purposes shall be considered to support water-dependent activities.*

For as long as those private commercial activities remain of a water-dependent nature, they shall be assessed at a sum reflecting the current use of said lands, and shall not be assessed at a rate that reflects the highest-and-best use of those lands.

The provisions of this section shall be applicable only to a county, city, or a municipality, which has adopted a local law or a school district that has adopted a resolution for the abatements provided herein.

Recommendation #29:

FINANCIAL AND TECHNICAL ASSISTANCE FOR MARINA AND BOATYARD ENVIRONMENTAL INFRASTRUCTURE IMPROVEMENTS SHOULD BE PROVIDED

Background

BECAUSE OF THEIR location at the land-sea interface, marinas, boatyards and other boating facilities on the East End must meet some of the strictest environmental standards in their operations. They have to meet federal, state and local regulatory requirements that don't apply to inland businesses. For small commercial marine operations, the cost of infrastructure improvements can be substantial ranging from $10,000 to install and operate a pumpout facility to $150,000 or more to modify area drainage systems and replace fuel tanks.

In many cases, it is difficult, if not impossible, for commercial facilities to recoup the cost of these modifications. The cumulative impact of environmental mandates is seriously eroding the profitability of small operations and driving some out of business altogether. Impending federal/state regulatory programs aimed at addressing coastal stormwater point source (under EPA's NPDES program) and non-point source (Section 6217(g) of the Coastal Zone Re-authorization Act of 1990) pollution clearly indicate the cost of environmental compliance for waterfront boating facilities will only increase in the near future.

Congress recognized the economic plight of the marine industry when it passed the Clean Vessel Act of 1992 which provides funds to the states to install boat sewage pumpout facilities. Grants are made on a competitive basis and priority is given to those states proposing public/private financing partnerships to encourage the installation of facilities.

In many cases, the sophistication of the myriad regulatory requirements and available best management practices for pollution abatement is beyond the technical expertise of the average small facility owner. Programs, such as the New York Sea Grant Extension, have been effective in providing marina operators with technical and education assistance in the area of environmentally sound facility design and operation, but resources for these efforts are limited and cannot meet the demand. If waterfront businesses are to implement pollution control requirements in an environmentally and economically effective manner, they will need increased technical and educational as well as financial assistance.

Proposed Action by the Governor:

1. The Governor should establish a grant or low-interest revolving loan program under the UDC, JDA or other appropriate agency to assist small marinas and other water-dependent businesses in making the infrastructure improvements they need to comply with environmental mandates. Administration of this program could be modeled after the Fisherman's Assistance Fund and the Fisheries Shoreside and Infrastructure Development Assistance Program proposed elsewhere in this report.

2. The Governor should direct the DEC and DOS to ensure that Federal Clean Vessel Act grant moneys are made available to any private facility that is mandated to have a pumpout facility as a result of state regulations or permits.

3. The Governor should formally appoint a Recreational Marine Industry Regulatory and Resource Advisory Council similar in structure and form to the DEC's Marine Resources Advisory Council. Presently, the DEC has the Marine Resources Advisory Council which is composed of recreational and commercial fishermen to advise them on state actions involving marine resources. There is no formal state level representation for the commercial recreational boating industry. The proposed committee would fill this void.

4. The Governor should support and expand technical assistance and education programs, such as the New York Sea Grant Program, which focus on helping the marine industry comply with environmental regulations while maintaining economic competitiveness.

Recommendation #30:

THE PERMIT SYSTEM FOR MARINAS SHOULD BE STREAMLINED AND SIMPLIFIED

Background

TO REMAIN COMPETITIVE, marinas must have the flexibility to change and expand to meet a shifting demand. A study entitled "North Atlantic Water-Dependent Use Study: Managing the Shoreline for Water-Dependent Use" done by the Maine Marine Law Institute for the New England/New York Coastal Task Force found that:

> "The most successful marinas are large and diversified selling and servicing boats, as well as storing them. Smaller marinas that can't increase to an efficient size are less well off."

Unfortunately, the small marina operator's ability to upgrade or expand to maintain economic viability is often thwarted by an unnecessarily complex, lengthy, and costly permit system. According to the State Office of Business Permits and Regulatory Assistance, a typical East End marina may be required to get over 30 separate permits and licenses from the state alone to do business. Agencies with jurisdiction include the DEC, DOS, DOH and OGS. Twenty different permits from the Department of Environmental Conservation may be needed. Additional approvals and permits are required from local and federal entities.

Lack of communication and coordination between and often within these agencies results in duplication of effort, overlapping jurisdictions, contradictory findings, unreasonable permit delays and extremely lengthy delays in obtaining approval for even simple projects. There are instances where facility owners have in good faith spent two to five years and tens of thousands of dollars trying to obtain Tidal Wetlands permits.

To avoid problems like this, other states have developed a number of different permitting strategies that should be considered in New York. Virginia has a true "one-stop" permit application and review program for wetlands and coastal projects where the applicant fills out one form and the state coordinates joint processing and decision meetings once a month between all the local, state and federal regulatory interests. These meetings are also used to serve as comprehensive preapplication conferences for potential project sponsors to identify potential problems and alternatives early in the process. Washington State has instituted similar regularly scheduled monthly meetings with state and federal interests.

In addition, because of the permit application fee structure set up for the Tidal Wetlands regulations, East End marinas pay state application fees 18 to 20 times higher than the fees charged for similar projects upstate. Under the State Protection of Waters and Freshwater Wetlands Programs, which cover marina activities above the Tappan Zee Bridge, applicants pay a $10 application fee for minor projects and $25 to $50 for a major project. Under Tidal Wetlands, an East End marina would have to pay an application fee of between $200 and $900 for the exact same activity.

Proposed Action by the Governor:

1. The Governor should implement Recommendations 1 and 2 in the section entitled "Simplifying the Regulatory Process" of the report from the Governor's Task Force on Coastal Resources (pp. 34-38).

The Governor should direct the DEC to initiate a joint permit application and review process for Tidal Wetlands permits for water-dependent use projects on the East End. The DEC should immediately develop a MOU with the Corps of Engineers Permitting Branch and develop a permit review committee consisting of representatives of the Department's Division of Regulatory Affairs, Bureau of Marine Habitat Protection and Corps personnel that will formally meet once a month to jointly process and review water-dependent use permits.

2. The Governor should direct the DEC to revise the Tidal Wetlands permit application fee structure for water-dependent businesses so that it matches the fees charged for similar projects under the DEC's Protection of Waters and Freshwater Wetlands programs. If additional funds are needed, application fees for all three programs should be adjusted accordingly.

3. The Governor should appoint a standing advisory committee composed of representatives of the East End marina industry, state regulatory agencies and the Governor's Office to monitor, identify and offer suggestions for correcting problems with the permitting process.

4. The Governor should direct the DEC Marine Resources Division and the Division of Regulatory Affairs to give priority to water-dependent businesses in coordinating and scheduling pre-application conferences for projects requiring Tidal Wetlands permits.

Recommendation #31:

RECENT AMENDMENTS TO THE NAVIGATION LAW SHOULD BE REVISED TO ASSURE EQUITABLE ACCESS TO COASTAL WATERS FOR ALL NEW YORK RESIDENTS

Background

JUST AS THE ROADS and highways on land allow the population to move freely around the state, our coastal waterways are the main thoroughfares for New York boaters. These waterways provide the access that allows millions of New Yorkers to enjoy our marine resources. Open access to the waters for all New York State residents is an important part of the public trust and crucial to the East End's economy and the general quality of life.

To maintain this access, it is important that transient navigation rights are not abridged by a patchwork of inconsistent, contradictory rules and regulations at the local level. Just as the state oversees the rules and regulations regarding travel on our roadways to safeguard the rights of the motorist, similar oversight is needed to insure that local laws are, indeed, in conformance with state and federal navigation laws and that inter- and intra-state commerce and travel are not unduly restricted.

This oversight used to be provided for under Section 46 of the Navigation Law, which called for review of local laws affecting navigation by the Commissioner of the Office of Parks, Recreation & Historic Preservation. This provision did not require a financial commitment by the localities. Unfortunately, this provision was revoked by recent legislation (Assembly Bill 8836 and Senate Bill 6182) which offered to relieve municipalities of costly state mandates. The portions of this legislation revising the Navigation Law do not provide any significant financial relief to local governments and seriously threaten the access and navigation right of New York's citizens.

Proposed Action by the Governor:

THE GOVERNOR SHOULD call for new legislation that mandates municipalities to submit their local navigation law regulations to the OPRHP Commissioner for approval, or call for legislation that assures the equitable use of New York waterways, which would guarantee boater's rights of free navigation in public waters, the right to incidental anchoring, harbors of safe refuge, and the choice to use a vessel of their own choosing.

TOURISM

Recommendation #32:

A TOURIST PLAN FOR THE EAST END SHOULD BE JOINTLY FUNDED BY THE STATE AND LOCAL GOVERNMENTS

Background

STRATEGIC PLANNING SUGGESTS communities should draw on their unique historical strengths when setting a course for a future. On the East End, it is the rural character, a high-quality environment, a heritage rich in Native American and Colonial culture, open spaces and vistas of land and water which support and nourish the industries of agriculture, fishing and tourism. The focus for economic development must be to sustain these industries in a way which is protective of our environment, cultural heritage and quality of life.

The sensitivity of the environmental quality that is the foundation of the region's economy also limits quantitative growth options. Efforts for development should concentrate on emerging patterns of increased year-round residents who commute to western Suffolk or retire to the area and second-home owners who might extend their seasonal enjoyment of their get-away place or use new communications technology to telecommute. The East End should increase efforts to position itself as a year-round recreation destination for the metropolitan region.

> "The truth is the more a community does to enhance its unique set of assets, whether natural, architectural, or cultural, the more tourists it will attract...Make a destination more appealing, and people will stay longer."
> Edward T. McMahon, *see* Appendix K.

The State should invest in the East End's future by assisting in the coordinated development and preservation of environmental, recreational, historic and cultural sites and facilities that are season-extending and year-round tourist destinations.

This plan would undertake to study the following recreational, cultural and historical proposals:

1. Public Golf Courses

Recent reports prepared by the Suffolk County Planning Department project an increase in the demand by the public to play golf on the East End. Opportunities exist to develop public golf courses at the Bridgehampton Racetrack and LILCO's Jamesport property, making golf more readily available to the general public.

There are 14 public golf courses on the East End. On average (in season), 300 people play per day. Most courses require reservations, others operate on a first-come-first served basis. Best informed estimates are that all of the courses are used to capacity on a daily basis. For example, Montauk Downs State Park has an average 4-to-5-hour wait in the summer.

Montauk Downs is the only State-owned/operated course on the East End. Revenue estimates are as follows:

> Open April to December (9 months); 9 months x 30 days = 270 days per year x 300 players per day = 31,000 players x $17 (average cost per day per player) = $1,377,000 in revenues generated annually.

2. Public Barrier Beach and Nature Preserve

The Fire Island National Seashore should be expanded to include Cupsogue County Park and an incorporated section of Dune Road. Two sections of the Dune Road Barrier Beach should be targeted for public purchase. The first is the property from Little Pike's Inlet to the Cupsogue County Park. The second is the two-mile stretch west of Suffolk County's holdings in East Quogue and Hampton Bays which includes the Great Dune. A Great Dune Nature Preserve should be established with two-to-three miles of natural, uninhabited beach. Existing structures and utility poles would be removed and replaced by an interpretative and limited-capacity recreational path and natural-setting boardwalks similar to Sunken Forest National Park. A platform tent facility run by the Park Service might be included. Access to these new park areas would be from roads at the borders of the parks and possibly by ferries in Eastport and East Quogue. State and/or federal acquisitions and operations would achieve two significant public goals—access to the ocean by the general public and season-extending operations to increase the area's attractiveness as an off-season tourist destination.

3. 1998 Goodwill Games

The East End should be seriously considered for several competitive venues during the 1998 Goodwill Games. As the state's premiere summer tourism destination, venues on the East End would enhance the image of the games and promote a vital industry. Venues which should be considered include swimming, rowing, kayaking (kayak course could be constructed at Splish Splash), and biking. (Note: Kayak slalom facility would extend Splish Splash season; see Appendix M.)

4. Comprehensive Recreational Trail Plan

Request funding to plan a region-wide, integrated system of bridle paths, hiking trails and bike paths (*see*, Recommendation #27 regarding bike paths). Funding sources include ISTEA, National Park Service and N.Y.S. DEC. Elements of funding should address promotion and location and interpretive signage. This plan should be written as a component of an overall tourism enhancement strategy for the region.

5. Heritage Tourism Development

N.Y.S. Parks & Recreation, Division of Historic Preservation should help develop a regional heritage tourism plan that includes Native American cultural sites, historic colonial sites and buildings and the Railroad Museum of Long Island. This plan should be written as a component of an overall tourism plan for the region.

6. Preservation of the East End Maritime Heritage and Restoration of Greenport's Deep-Water Harbor Facilities

The East End of Long Island has had an important maritime heritage that goes back to the late 1700's, and especially during the 1800's with principal ports being Greenport and Sag Harbor. Greenport was noted for its shipbuilding industry. A comprehensive detailed plan to promote Greenport's deep-water port with enhancement of its local museums, tall ships, and other marine activities should be pursued. Details of this plan are set forth in Appendix O.

7. Railroad Museum of Long Island

The Railroad Museum of Long Island was chartered by the New York Board of Regents in 1990. It is located in Greenport and Riverhead. The museum is completing the restoration of the Greenport Freight Station which has been the eastern terminal for the Long Island Railroad since 1844. The Long Island Railroad Rolling Stock Collection contains ten pieces including a 1907 snow plow, one of the two remaining steam locomotives, and the first double-decker built in 1932. This collection is located in Riverhead. The trustees and officers of the museum have identified several projects and capital improvements that would enable the Railroad Museum to operate on a year-round basis and should be considered part of the tourist plan. They are set forth in attached Appendix P.

Proposed Action by the Governor:

THE GOVERNOR SHOULD request the Office of Economic Development with other agencies to jointly fund with the five East End Towns the development of a Regional Tourist Plan for the East End.

Recommendation #33:

THE "I LOVE NY" CAMPAIGN SHOULD PROMOTE THE EAST END

Background

THE EAST END IS an ideal vacation spot for tourists and daytrippers. The many diverse activities found here form the basis for the area's tourist-driven economy. The East End's economy and employment of area residents could be enhanced dramatically through proper tourism promotion.

A report entitled, "Promoting Tourism and Business Travel on Long Island, A Plan for the Future, 1990," identified a number of significant points, in particular,

> "Tourism is not an automatic growth industry for Long Island; it must be carefully nurtured to produce acceptable growth rates."

The same study identified a series of opportunities which will provide for multi-season tourism development. They are: 1) recreational fishing tournaments, 2) winery tours, 3) sports events (golf and tennis tournaments), 4) maritime harbor festival, 5) air shows (cradle of aviation), 6) county fairs, 7) high-tech fairs, 8) performing art promotions, 9) historical tours, 10) fall apple/pumpkin festival, 11) self-improvement seminars, and 12) aquarium sitings.

Some of these events would lend themselves as season extenders for the East End. Yet, for some of them to happen, additional state promotion funds are necessary.

The New York State Department of Economic Development spends over $2 million annually for media production and campaigns in the I Love NY program (*see*, Appendix N). This campaign primarily highlights upstate New York and New York City.

The "I Love NY" Matching Funds program has awarded $150,000 to the Long Island Convention and Visitors Bureau which serves as the agent to promote Long Island tourism. The LICVB then seeks funding throughout the Long Island community to match the $150,000 state grant. Best estimates are that approximately $25,000 of this state grant is available for direct eastern Long Island campaigns and promotional literature.

The "I Love NY" Matching Funds program is awarded based on a formula that is not favorable to Long Island. Grants are awarded based on the number of counties which participate in regional campaigns. Long Island applies for grants under Nassau and Suffolk. Regions like the Finger Lakes, which have 14 counties, have received $6.5 million in grants compared to $1.8 million for Long Island over the last 19 years. This funding formula is unfair to Long Island and should be revised.

Proposed Action by the Governor:

THE GOVERNOR SHOULD direct the Department of Economic Development to focus more attention in the I Love NY program to the East End. Specifically, an additional $200,000 grant should be given to Long Island, earmarked for East End tourism promotion to be matched by the five East End Towns.

Recommendation #34:

THE 5% LUXURY TAX ON HOTELS SHOULD BE REPEALED

Background

THIS TAX WAS INSTITUTED in June of 1990 and has been a source of controversy ever since. The purpose of the tax is to help "balance the budget" in New York State and goes into the General Fund.

On the East End of Long Island, there are over 5,800 hotel rooms, 4,163 of which are "seasonal." A large proportion of these rooms (2,036) are in the Town of East Hampton (Montauk Motel/Hotel Industry). The season here on the East End is basically from May to October, three months of which are considered "peak season." The other months are marginal, at best, and, indeed, operators are lucky to "break even" and pay expenses in these months. Many of these motel operations are small and cannot bear the yoke of the added 5% tax.

Although, ostensibly, the vacationer bears the cost of this tax, motel operators have found that their guests object strenuously, often resulting in shorter stays and no repeat business. The motel operators often have to absorb the tax themselves, hence, the deluge of $99.99 rooms which keeps them under the taxable amount of $100 or over. Any vacationer from New York City, Nassau County, or Western Suffolk can easily go to Pennsylvania, New Jersey, Massachusetts, or indeed, the Bahamas, where the tax is much less.

A study done by the New York State Hospitality Tourism Association and the Hotel Association of New York City bears out the "economic kick" to the industry statewide. The study concludes that the $63 million generated from this room tax results in a loss of $158 million in other taxes annually [**reference the Study**]. It has succeeded in lowering room rates, alienating the vacationer, and preventing operators from maintaining and upgrading their establishments. When labor, fuel costs, and operating expenses are escalating, it is hardly logical that room rates should go down in price. The trickle-down effect of this tax reaches into all retail businesses, restaurants, charter boats, retail shops, etc.

The tax is particularly unfair in a resort area, such as the East End, where the economy is based on a three-month peak season and there is no opportunity to do the volume of business that might offset its burdensome effects.

Proposed Action by the Governor:

THE GOVERNOR SHOULD introduce legislation to repeal this tax or exempt the East End from this tax.

Recommendation #35:

THE JOBS DEVELOPMENT AUTHORITY SHOULD BE AUTHORIZED TO ENABLE TOURISM FACILITIES TO BENEFIT

Background

MANY OF LONG ISLAND'S travel-related businesses are small, family-owned firms. They have difficulty raising capital for improvements or expansion because commercial banks consider such loans too risky.

Eastern Long Island has no major manufacturing firms, no heavy industry and no large or major employers.

The Eastern Long Island Tourist industry consists mainly of relatively small accommodation facilities, restaurants and retail stores. These facilities employ most of eastern Long Island seasonal employees and represent a major portion of the Long Island job market.

At present, State Department of Economic Development (DED) funding is not available to overnight lodging facilities or retail stores and thus most of Eastern Long Island's tourist economy is not eligible for DED funding.

In the past several years, State Department of Economic Development funding of between $1.125 million and $2.5 million has been available for tourism facility financing. During the July 1988-89 period, the New York Business Development Corporation, a quasi-private bank, dispersed nearly $9.2 million to help finance qualified tourism operations. However, none of these funds were available for overnight lodging or retail stores.

Tourism projects may also be financed through the New York State Urban Development Corporation's Regional Economic Development Partnership Program ("REDPP"). Eligible projects include tourist destination facilities that are not *overnight lodging or retail stores*. A tourism destination is defined as a location or facility which is likely to attract a significant number of visitors from outside the region. Preference is given to projects attracting a significant number of visitors from out of state.

The Job Development Authority, which provides favorable incentives to businesses with the objective of creating jobs, is not presently allowed by the New York State Constitution to assist tourist-related industries thereby denying assistance to tourism and related facilities.

Eligible projects that could benefit from an amended JDA would include the expansion and modernization of Eastern Long Island's aging accommodation facilities and thus provide additional jobs for the area. Restaurants could be enlarged and new jobs created. Retail establishments could plan on longer and expanded periods of employment thus creating additional employment opportunities. The modernization and expansion of Long Island Infrastructure would help make possible the extension of the "tourist season" and aid in establishing a year-round economy for Eastern Long Island.

At present, the only funding programs available to Eastern Long Island's tourist industry do not provide assistance to lodging, restaurants or retail establishments.

Proposed Action by the Governor:

THE GOVERNOR SHOULD renew his request to the State Legislature to commence the constitutional amendment procedure necessary to permit the Job Development Authority to assist tourist-related industries to allow low-interest loans and loan guarantees to assist companies in expanding facilities and building new facilities.

Recommendation #36:

A MARKETING SURVEY TO IDENTIFY POTENTIAL MARKETS AND VISITORS' NEEDS AND MAXIMIZE BENEFITS DERIVED FROM TOURISM ADVERTISING DOLLARS SHOULD BE JOINTLY FUNDED

Background

THE TOTAL TOURISM INDUSTRY on Long Island is estimated to be approximately $2.5 billion annually, of which 40% (or $1 billion) is attributed to the East End.

In June, July and August of 1993 extrapolation of ¾% hotel tax estimates more than $55 million was spent on lodging alone on the East End. Considering a 1.8 money multiplier effect, the three-month lodging figure is $100 million.

A survey and marketing study should be conducted to learn more about the origins and needs of the East End tourist. No such study has ever been done. Once completed, the study would enable the Towns and State to better build this important job-producing industry. Such a survey could be prepared by Suffolk Community College Center for Community Research. A budget of $50,000 is needed.

Proposed Action by the Governor:

THE GOVERNOR SHOULD direct the Department of Economic Development to undertake such a jointly funded study with the five East End Towns.

Recommendation #37:

TOURIST INFORMATION CENTERS SHOULD BE ESTABLISHED

Background

EACH YEAR, over 600,000 people enter the East End through Orient Point alone. This is an excellent opportunity to acquaint visitors with all of the cultural and natural resources and other tourist-related activities.

Tourism information centers are vital to maximize traveler expenditures and help ensure repeat tourism business. They welcome New York state travelers, direct them appropriately and encourage them to see and do more while here. As tourism industry representatives have often pointed out, New York State is the only eastern seaboard state lacking information centers to welcome travelers at its borders.

Two categories of information centers are recommended for Eastern Long Island: (1) a Gateway Information Center, possibly at Orient, and (2) Destination Information Centers on both forks. Such centers would help to achieve a coordinated statewide tourism information system and develop guidelines, policies and technical tourism-related services for the system.

In 1986, the State Legislature appropriated $2 million for planning and construction of several centers at major entrances to the state.

The Department of Economic Development ("DED") staff assembles programmatic, operational and equipment budgets. DED develops collateral materials, videos, regional displays, etc. through its own resources and those of the State Education Department and the State Office of Parks, Recreation and Historic Preservation. The DOT is ultimately responsible for the design and construction of gateway information centers.

Several Information Centers to provide visitors with information on destination attractions, events and appropriate routing, include transportation centers, regional interpretive centers, county information centers and some major tourism attractions should be established. A regional map of the entire East End would be produced.

Possible locations include the Long Island Expressway and the Sunrise Highway near western boundaries of the Towns of Riverhead and Southampton and the Port Jefferson and Orient areas in order to serve ferry visitors from Connecticut. The additional centers would help mitigate visitor complaints about inadequate information concerning Long Island's travel-related facilities, particularly those that remain open in the off-season.

Increased attention should also be given to signage on Long Island roads, hiking trails, beaches, and other tourist facilities. Signs in these areas should be reviewed for clarity, accuracy and consistency.

Proposed Action by the Governor:

THE GOVERNOR SHOULD direct the Department of Economic Development to establish a Gateway Information Center at Orient Point and East End Tourist Information Centers at the appropriate locations.

REGIONAL ISSUES

Recommendation #38:

THE CREATION OF AN EAST END EDUCATION CENTER AT THE EASTERN CAMPUS OF SUFFOLK COMMUNITY COLLEGE SHOULD BE FURTHER STUDIED

Background

A RECURRING THEME of the Task Force's report is the distinct rural character of the five East End Towns. Important organizations in rural communities typically lack the economies of scale present in more urbanized areas to provide efficient services to citizens. In the case of Suffolk County, the problem is exacerbated by suburban policy makers who view our rural community needs as comparatively insignificant and costly. As a result, the community college campus in Riverhead remains incomplete after fifteen years, BOCES I is merged with its suburban counterpart to the west and Cornell Cooperative Extension is housed in inadequate quarters. Given the authority, its likely that the East End officials and their organizations would respond to this challenge the way many rural communities do—work collaboratively to meet the pressing and unique needs of their citizens.

The Community College, BOCES' Harry B. Ward Occupational Education Center in Riverhead, and Cornell Cooperative Extension of Suffolk serve the same region with similar and overlapping educational missions. With its location and record of collaboration and cooperation, there is strong programmatic and economic logic for establishing a regional education center at the Eastern Campus. The general concept of this center is to bring the public educational institutions that service the East End together on the Eastern Campus so that regional educational and economic development needs are available at one location.

Cornell Cooperative Extension

THE FIRST STEP in meeting that goal would be locating the Suffolk County Cooperative Extension at the Eastern Campus. Both organizations would benefit immensely from this physical proximity. There are many programmatic similarities between the academic offerings of the Community College and the continuing education and economic development mission of the

Cornell Cooperative Extension. Both institutions have educational programs which focus on horticulture, marine science and dietetics.

The benefits for a common location are also economic. The infrastructure of the Eastern Campus—its parking lot, sewer system, heating plant, and water system—were built to accommodate eight-to-ten buildings. Constructing a facility for another agency on the Campus would allow the College to reduce the overhead costs of maintaining these presently underutilized capital investments. The availability of these utilities should reduce the basic construction costs for the new Cooperative Extension facility. In -addition, the Cooperative Extension need not include in their plans the classrooms and auditorium it might require if located elsewhere. Likewise, the Cooperative Extension could potentially provide lab and studio space for Community College programs, while using college interns and cooperative education students to supplement its educational services.

BOCES

SIMILAR BENEFITS are derived from locating the vocational education facilities of the Ward Tech Center on the campus. BOCES and the Eastern Campus share several educational missions, including local economic development, vocational education, enrichment programming and adult literacy. Because of these common missions, program development followed similar paths. Both the college and BOCES have academic programs in business, computers, office technology, restaurant management, horticulture and graphic design. Special facilities for these curriculums are now provided at two locations within four miles of each other. Greenhouses and special instructional laboratories for computers, food preparation, graphic design and adult literacy and remedial skills exist at both the Eastern Campus and Harry B. Ward Occupational Education Center.

Occupational education programs provide the richest opportunities for program coordination and facility and equipment sharing between the college and BOCES. In this area of programming, the Harry B. Ward Occupational Center has superior equipment and facilities. The make-shift cooking laboratory in the college cafeteria and the temporary greenhouses at the campus do not compare to the multi-station culinary laboratory for the restaurant management program and the extensive, fully equipped greenhouses for the horticulture program at the Ward Tech Center. Scheduling restrictions inherent in high school programming leave these facilities idle part of the day. The college program could easily be scheduled around the BOCES' restaurant management program, resulting in a better-utilized facility. Similar circumstances exist for the horticulture and graphic design programs of BOCES and the college. Coordinated use of the greenhouses and design labs would easily accommodate college and high school programs. In addition, the new site at the college campus would offer the opportunity to create demonstration plots for nursery stock production, vineyard cultivation and lawn and garden care for training in these expanding eastern Long Island industries.

East End Environmental Education & Tourism Center

A FINAL SUGGESTION for the regional education center at Eastern Campus is the establishment of an East End Environmental Education and Tourism Center. Modeled after three facilities developed upstate in the Catskills and Adirondack Mountains, these interpretive centers are "constructed n park areas of the state to introduce visitors to the culture, history, geology, ecology and economics of a region as well as to its scenic attractions" ("$5 Million Center is Planned for the Catskills," by Harold Faber, *New York Times*, May 15, 1988, p. 44). In explaining the importance of a $5 million state-financed facility in Shandaken in Ulster County, Governor Cuomo commented, "The Catskill Center will foster a sense of regional identity, encourage tourism and appropriate economic development, and increase understanding of the importance of protecting this great natural resource." The Governor's words apply with equal force to the need for a facility on the eastern end of Long Island. The New York State, Suffolk County and eastern Long Island towns have invested heavily in land and ecosystem preservation on the East End. Full return on this investment will not accrue until this magnificent park and preserve system capitalizes on its recreation and tourism potential. An interpretive center is necessary to insure the sensitive public use of this public investment.

Locating an environmental and tourism facility at the East End Regional Education Center gives it an advantage not afforded its upstate counterparts. Existing and planned curriculums at BOCES and the college, and the program areas of Cornell Cooperative Extension offer the faculty expertise and student-intern resources that can provide cost-effective programming opportunities to the general public and a unique learning laboratory for students. A variety of internship and other academic experiences would become available through this center. Environmental science students could write trail guides, landscape management students could design and build the trails, graphic design students make the interpretive signs for the trails and hospitality and tourism students could work at the center during special events and promotions. Finally, Cornell Cooperative Extension, BOCES, and the college would collaborate to provide environmental and conservation education to Long Island school districts. This service would be tailored to compliment programming at the BOCES III Outdoor Learning Center in Smithtown. It would offer unique experiences in marine science and fill a science programming void on the East End.

Pine Barrens Commission

ADDING TO THE WEIGHT of evidence supporting the concept of a regional education center at the Community College's Riverhead Campus is the desire of the newly created Pine Barrens Commission to locate its headquarters at the campus. In one of its first official actions, the Commission passed a resolution designating the Community College Campus as its preferred future home. The offices of this important new regional agency, along with computer facilities and research library, could be housed in the East End Environmental and Tourism Center.

In summary, the proposal to form a regional education center that includes Cornell Cooperative Extension of Suffolk, the Harry B. Ward Occupational Education Center and the East End Environmental Education and Tourism Center at the Eastern Campus of Suffolk Community College would consolidate a number of state-funded institutions and services at a convenient, cost-effective location. This proposal offers gains both in the quality of educational programs and in the economic development services for the East End. Despite the compelling arguments for implementation, however, it crosses so many institutional and political boundaries that only the good graces of the Governor's Office could make it a reality. To proceed with the Regional Education Center concept, the East End Economic and Environmental Task Force requests that the Governor establish a working committee of SUNY Central and State Education Department officials, state and county legislators from eastern Long Island, and administrators from Suffolk Community College, BOCES and Cornell Cooperative Extension of Suffolk to create a plan for shared facilities at the campus. Chair of the New York State Senate Education Committee, Ken LaValle, who is familiar with elements of the concept, might be asked to lead this study group. One of the charges of this committee would explore funding for the facilities to complete the center, including a variety of state, county and local capital budgets, including the Urban Development Corporation for the Environmental Education and Tourism Center.

Proposed Action by the Governor:

THE GOVERNOR SHOULD create a study group to analyze the cost and benefits to the East End of the creation of an East End Education Center at the Eastern Campus of Suffolk Community College.

Recommendation #39:

FAIRNESS AND FLEXIBILITY FOR UNIVERSITY MEDICAL CENTER AT STONY BROOK SHOULD BE ENACTED

Background

THE THREE STATE UNIVERSITY Hospitals, including the University Medical Center at Stony Brook, are disadvantaged by a system of antiquated laws, regulations and administrative restrictions in a rapidly changing health care marketplace.

The University Medical Center at Stony Brook, which has a particularly critical relationship with East Enders and our community hospitals—especially through the regional trauma care network facilitated by Stony Brook and the five East End Towns—is directly impacted by the present statutory set up.

The four areas of need of the SUNY Hospitals which must be addressed in the upcoming legislative session deal with:

    a) access to capital
    b) reliable use and access to reserve funds
    c) increased delegation of authority for purchasing/contracting
    d) pay equity for nurses

A) *Access to Capital*—Every hospital in New York State, with the exception of the three SUNY hospitals, has access to capital for purchasing expensive medical equipment or updating facilities through a state agency called the Medical Care Facility Finance Association (MCFFA). The University Medical Center at Stony Brook and the other SUNY hospitals are simply seeking fairness and equality of treatment with other hospitals on this issue. Without the ability to access capital through MCFFA, Stony Brook is at a competitive disadvantage in the present health care environment.

B) *Reserve Funds*—Stony Brook and other SUNY hospitals need to have reliable access to their own funds—that is, revenue that has been generated by the Medical Center itself. Reserve funds reimbursement can be altered by relatively small changes in the State Department of Health's reimbursement methodology.

C) *Purchasing*—The University Medical Center needs to be able to purchase equipment essential to its operation in a much faster fashion. Presently, the limit on purchases for goods and materials is $50,000. With the skyrocketing cost of high-tech medical equipment over the past several years, SUNY is seeking an increase in that limit to $250,000.

D) *Parity for Nurses*—Nurses at the University Medical Center at Stony Brook are the lowest paid on Long Island with their salaries capped after three years. Lower salaries and longer work weeks have caused Stony Brook's nurses (the most highly trained in the region) to leave the Medical Center in record numbers—a 27% turnover rate alone, during the past year, a rate more than five times the turnover rate throughout the Northeast. Stony Brook's nurses are going to private hospitals to earn from $4,000 to $17,000 more and to private nursing agencies, which then lease back the services of those very same nurses to Stony Brook at a much higher cost to the hospital.

Proposed Action by the Governor:

TO SURVIVE AND better serve the East End community in the new managed care/health care environment on Long Island, the University Medical Center at Stony Brook needs specific legislation enacted to remedy the problem areas cited above.

1. *Enacting legislation which gives the three SUNY Medical Centers parity and flexibility*. The areas of access to capital, reliable use and access to revenue funds and an increase in delegation of authority for contracting are practical issues properly addressed in SUNY Central's proposed "Flexibility" legislation.
   We urge the Governor to embrace the SUNY Central proposals as part of his own program bill to enable Stony Brook and the other SUNY hospitals to better serve the citizens in their regions of the State. Existing legislation (S6212 sponsored by Senator LaValle and A8665 sponsored by Assemblyman Ed Sullivan) could be conformed with a comprehensive Governor's program bill that reflects the clear goals of greater business-like flexibility for SUNY's hospitals.

2. *Enacting legislation which gives the nurses at SUNY Stony Brook pay and benefit parity with nurses at other Long Island Hospitals*. Senator Jim Lack introduced legislation during the last legislative session which would have resolved the nurses' pay parity issue for Stony Brook nurses. We urge the Governor to support the critically important Lack bill for nurses' pay parity (Senate Bill 3600-A). Its passage is essential for the University Medical Center to continue to provide the highest quality health care services for East Enders and all Long Islanders.

Recommendation #40:

WORKER'S COMPENSATION REFORM SHOULD BE ADOPTED

Background

THE COST OF worker's compensation in New York State has become an unbearable burden on East End employers. New York State's businesses now pay almost $5 billion annually for worker's compensation, which is as much as all New York business taxes combined. Worker's compensation insurance premiums have increased more than 60% for the average New York business over the last three years and more than 90% over the last five years. The result has been and will continue to be the loss of jobs. East End employers cannot continue to shoulder these burdensome costs.

Worker's compensation safety groups have seen their insurance premiums double. For example, premiums in New York Farm Bureau's Worker's Compensation Safety Group went from a total of $6.25 million in 1987 to $12.81 million in 1991. Individual employers have witnessed even greater increases. The latest increase of 17.1% in 1993 was a record sixth straight increase in worker's compensation insurance rates.

An affordable worker's compensation system, which pays for legitimate work place injuries, is possible because other states have already made necessary reforms. States like Oregon have achieved substantial efficiency in their programs. Unlike New York, injury claims in Oregon have fallen 17% and employer premiums have dropped by nearly 30% since 1990. In fact, the savings have been significant enough that benefits for more serious injuries have been increased, making Oregon's program a recruiting device. Other states such as Colorado, Florida, and most recently Maine, have made the hard choices necessary to keep worker's compensation an affordable, viable system to take care of employees injured on the job.

Provide Managed Care

THE COST OF TREATING work place injuries should be controlled through the use of managed care. It is estimated that 36 cents out of every dollar in worker's compensation payments in New York goes toward medical care. Medical costs for worker's compensation have increased at twice the rate of medical costs. Currently, medical care is being used by virtually every industry and level of government to moderate health care cost increases, yet is not allowed under New York's worker's compensation law. The savings from switching to managed care have been estimated at anywhere from 5% to 25% of the health care bill. Using an average savings of 15%, managed care could potentially save more than $189 million a year in unnecessary premiums.

Eliminate Third-Party Suits

IN ADDITION, the ability of a third party to sue an employer should be barred, which would void the *Dole v. Dow* court ruling. The Legislature should reaffirm the exclusive remedy principle that underlies the entire worker's compensation system. Legislative action would save New York employers an estimated $360 million annually in premiums (S 5886-C Lack).

Eliminate Duplicative Coverage

COSTLY OR FRAUDULENT practices should be eliminated. There is nothing in state law that precludes an employee, who is collecting worker's compensation while he is recuperating from an injury, to also file for and collect unemployment insurance. Income from other sources should be coordinated with the payment of worker's compensation indemnity benefits. Legislation is proposed which limits unemployment benefits that would be received while receiving worker's compensation (S 2028 Lack/A 4168 Schimminger). Legislation is also proposed which limits compensation benefits if the injury was sustained by an employee in the perpetration of an illegal act (S 3395 Lack/A 4208 Schimminger).

Eliminate Hospital Surcharge

ANOTHER COSTLY PRACTICE is the requirement that worker's compensation insurers pay a 13% surcharge for in-hospital care provided to worker's compensation claimants. Worker's compensation is not the product line for which the surcharge was necessary and, with the advent of community rating, there is no reason to continue the surcharge. It is estimated that employers could save up to 2.5% in worker's compensation rates with this single reform.

Create Farm Safety Education Program

WORK PLACE SAFETY must be further encouraged. Agricultural safety programs in New York, which are already effective at reducing work place injuries, include the activities of the New York State Rural Health and Safety

Council and the New York State Center for Agricultural Medicine and Health at Bassett Hospital. We support an initiative to establish a direct relationship between worker's compensation rates and a safe farm working environment. Specifically, we support the establishment of an incentive for farmers to correct human health hazards through a farm safety audit/safety education program. Under the auspices of the New York State Rural Health and Safety Council at Cornell University, this program would offer farmers an opportunity to earn a discount on worker's compensation rates provided they implement the recommendations of a certified farm safety audit and/or complete a certified farm course. This concept is parallel to the auto insurance discount awarded following completion of a certified defensive driving course.

Proposed Action by the Governor:

THE GOVERNOR SHOULD introduce and/or support S 5886-C, S 2028 and S 3395 and support the agricultural safety program.

Recommendation #41:

REASONABLE RETURN ON PROPERTY SHOULD BE RECOGNIZED IN STATE LEGISLATION

Background

THE INCENTIVE TO continue farming and hold on to farmland and own private lands and open space could be jeopardized if farmers or private landowners are penalized for maintaining open space for the benefit of society. Farmers have maintained farms and land for generations while withstanding the temptation of sale for development purposes. They are entitled to the security of knowing that government will not enact laws or implement regulations depriving them of a reasonable return on their property.

At the forefront is the Fifth Amendment of the U.S. Constitution which states "no person shall be deprived of life, liberty, or property without due process of law; nor shall private property be taken for public use without just compensation."

New York State government and agencies should be required to mitigate the impact on private property owners prior to enacting laws or promulgating rules and regulations which may result in a "taking" or the effect of a "taking."

Land use regulations that foster the effect of a "taking" are contrary to the goals of most community master plans. New York State should promote policies and regulations that will fulfill—not belie—regional preservation and economic goals.

Therefore, we recommend a bill to require state agencies, prior to taking regulatory action, to certify that the proposed action will not result in a taking of private property without just compensation. This certification and the basis thereof should be duly filed at the time the rule or regulation becomes effective.

Proposed Action by the Governor:

THE GOVERNOR SHOULD introduce legislation to implement the above.

Recommendation #42:

MANDATE RELIEF SHOULD BE ADOPTED

Background

STATE MANDATES POSE a great burden on property taxpayers. Suffolk County residents are facing continuing tax increases, a possible discontinuation of all other services except social services, or bankruptcy of county government because of state mandated programs. We cannot impress upon you enough the urgency of this problem. State mandates such as Medicaid, the Wicks Law, and landfill closure rules have produced a crisis in local government finances and it is local taxpayers who are victims. We strongly urge action to solve this problem this year.

The connection between farmers and state mandates is real property tax. Farmers lease or own approximately 30% of the land in the state as a necessary component of farming. Unfortunately, this means that any increases in the real property tax impact farmers disproportionately compared to other taxpayers. New York farmers are not only at a disadvantage compared to their fellow taxpayers, but also pay about twice the amount of real property taxes as their colleagues in competitive states. Property tax increases have been levied by county governments as a result of the increasing mandate burdens placed on county finances.

We recommend that real mandate reform be based on the following premises:

1) Cost containment of mandated programs in order to provide tax relief for the overburdened taxpayer.
2) Greater local control over mandated programs in order to reduce spiraling costs.
3) A more stable budgeting process at the local level.
4) Tax reduction and the reduction of unnecessary or overburdening regulations.
5) All state mandated programs, new or old, should be funded by the state.

County government in New York pays for as much as one-fourth of the total cost of Medicaid. New York is one of the few states that requires a local contribution to the cost of the program. Although counties have no control over the program, they are forced to help pay for the skyrocketing cost. Unable to control the increasing cost but forced to help pay for it, counties have resorted to seeking additional revenue through property tax increases. A recent Association of Counties survey revealed that on the average, counties will spend 57.7% of their 1993 budgets on state mandated programs. Many counties have an even higher percentage of their budgets devoted to mandates. Because county budgets are dominated by Medicaid and other mandated costs, localities have looked to property tax revenue for relief.

Medicaid costs have nearly doubled since 1987, while the caseload has risen 59% since then. Overall Medicaid expenses went from $54.5 million in 1987 to an estimated $102 million this year. Counties have little control over the Medicaid program. Their budgets are consumed by Medicaid-dominated, state-mandated expenses, and the increasing cost of the program may not be attributable wholly to an increased caseload. State management of Medicaid has contributed to the financial burden on localities and, therefore, to the tax burden on farmers.

Proposed Action by the Governor:

1) *Enacting legislation which prohibits future mandates without funding.* To begin to reform the way the state pays for programs using mandates, we must first stop the imposition of any additional, unfunded mandates upon local governments. The Association of Counties estimates that the state has shifted an additional $1.4 billion in unfunded mandates onto the backs of counties and local taxpayers as a result of the past three budgets.

2) *Enacting a state takeover of the local cost of Medicaid with cost containment.* Local taxpayers pay over $3 billion to help fund Medicaid in New York State. Medicaid is the largest and one of the fastest growing mandates on local governments and must be prioritized to change the way it is paid for and to control the rate of increase in cost. There is almost unanimous agreement that it is unfair for local taxes to be used to pay for Medicaid and that containment of Medicaid costs must accompany any state takeover of local costs. What is holding up passage of a state takeover plan is disagreement over how to contain the increasing cost of Medicaid.

Aggressive cost containment must accompany any takeover plan and any cost containment plan must aim to reduce the growth in the cost of Medicaid to a rate similar to the growth in state revenues. If Medicaid is allowed to grow at a rate higher than the rate of growth in state revenues, the result will be the need for annual tax increases at the state level as is happening locally now. Containing the annual increases in Medicaid costs to approximately the medical care component of the cost of living index is a worthy goal to aim for. New York is one of only three states to provide full optional services for Medicaid, resulting in health care coverage that is more extensive than private insurance.

A state takeover of the local cost of Medicaid with a reduction in the rate of growth in Medicaid costs must happen. On the average in 1993, over 38% of the county tax levies will be allocated to pay for Medicaid. New York taxpayers can no longer afford to help pay for Medicaid on a local level.

The Governor must be recognized for his leadership in preparing a plan to take over the local cost of Medicaid. Now, we ask that the Assembly, Senate and Governor's Office work together to negotiate a plan for Medicaid takeover which will control growth in medicaid costs by providing Medicaid services more efficiently and by considering the elimination of some optional services.

3) *Repealing the Wicks Law (A 3931/S 3941, A 2981/S 1768).* The Wicks Law is a series of laws which mandate that local governments manage multiple contractors for construction projects. It has been estimated that the Wicks Law mandate adds 20-30% to construction costs, costing local governments and taxpayers $400 million per year. If making the Wicks Law optional is not possible this year, the threshold for when the Wicks Law would be mandatory should be raised. Increasing the threshold would help local finances while protecting those projects which may be more at risk of corruption. The state's taxpayers need relief from this costly mandate this year.

Recommendation #43:

THE PROPOSED JETPORT AT CALVERTON SHOULD BE OPPOSED

Background

THE FAA HAS PROVIDED $400,000 to the Long Island Regional Planning Board to fund a feasibility study on the development of a jetport at Navy-owned property leased to the Grumman Corp. in Calverton which has been used for test flights of military aircraft on a periodic basis. This site lies in the heart of the Long Island pine barrens, is a State-designated Special Groundwater Protection Area, and lies within the Peconic River Corridor, the Pine Barrens-Maritime Reserve and the Peconic Estuary. The traditional industries of Long Island's East End towns and villages require the retention of rural qualities, the right to quiet enjoyment of property, and the preservation of our fragile environment. East End municipalities have expended millions of taxpayers' dollars to preserve the local environment through comprehensive plans designed to preserve the rural character and environmental health of the area. The proposed jetport would threaten the East End's tourism, farming and fishing-based economies and could result in declining property values, higher taxes and increased air and noise pollution.

The East End Supervisors and Mayors Association unanimously adopted a Resolution dated April 22, 1992 opposing the conversion of the Calverton facility to a commercial jetport for cargo or passenger aircraft.

Proposed Action by the Governor:

THE GOVERNOR SHOULD oppose the conversion of the Calverton facility to a commercial jetport for cargo or passenger aircraft in order to help preserve the rural character of the East End and its agricultural-, fishing- and second-home-based economies.

Recommendation #44:

MATCHING STATE FUNDING FOR STUDY OF FINANCIAL FEASIBILITY OF FORMING PECONIC COUNTY SHOULD BE SUPPORTED

Background

DURING THE PAST thirty years, the concept of combining the Towns of Riverhead, Southampton, East Hampton, Shelter Island, and Southold to form Peconic County has continued to appeal to East Enders as feelings of disenfranchisement from Suffolk County government have grown. There are a number of compelling reasons that serve to promote and enhance the concept of forming Peconic County.

The Towns of East Hampton, Riverhead, Shelter Island, Southampton and Southold, while part of Suffolk County, have clearly shown themselves to be a separate and distinct entity in many ways. First, as it has been well-documented throughout the Task Force's report, the East End is primarily rural in character compared with the suburban sprawl of western Suffolk. The population density of western Suffolk is nearly seven times' greater than the East End. Such diverse population demographics reflect not only a statistical difference, but translates into different economic bases, social problems, needs and goals for the future. In short, there is a different way of life on the East End.

Unlike western Suffolk, which possesses a largely commercial and industrial economic base, the East End depends on the preservation of its unique rural character and natural resources for its economic well-being. Clearly, the East End is still a region of small villages, rolling farm fields, pine barrens, beaches and wetlands. Specifically, tourism, recreation, the second home industry, agriculture and fishing remain the East End's economic base and depend heavily on the preservation of our natural resources.

Secondly, support for the formation of Peconic County has grown in the past few years as Suffolk County's fiscal condition has worsened. While the East End accounts for only 8% of the County's population, it pays nearly 25% of the general fund tax levy for Suffolk. The East End pays an estimated $12 million for County police services, even though all the East End municipalities possess their own departments.

In addition, increases in the sales tax and hotel taxes have proved to be a heavy burden for the East End tourist-based economy. While revenues collected by Suffolk County from the East End continue to increase, it is widely acknowledged that services have diminished. Since the East End has only two votes on the 18-member Suffolk County Legislature, it is not surprising that East End programs and services are the first to be slashed when County government seeks to cut costs.

Aside from all the substantive differences between western Suffolk and the East End that have been identified, the loss of home rule has dismayed the East End since the Board of Supervisors was declared illegal and replaced by an 18-member Legislature in 1970. Under the old system, the East End had 5 votes and western Suffolk had 5 votes, insuring that western Suffolk County could not undermine home rule and ignore East End needs.

However, under the current legislative system, the needs of the East End are always beholden to the western Suffolk majority. Simply stated, there is no home rule or self-determination on the East End, but dependence on the good will of western Suffolk. Accordingly, the profound demographic differences between western Suffolk and the East End create often conflicting demands on scarce government resources.

There are a number of significant reasons to believe that creating Peconic County may make good economic sense. First, if Peconic County were formed, it would be 5th of 57 counties outside New York City in property-tax base. In this regard, it is recognized that the Counties which generate the most sales tax revenue in the state per capital are areas with a tourist-based economy, such as the Lake George area and the Catskills. In fact, if Peconic County were formed, it would be second in New York in per capital sales revenue and larger than 39 other New York counties on the basis of population.

Furthermore, the East End does not wish to duplicate the structure of Suffolk County government with its high-price commissioners and excessive bureaucracy. For example, Peconic County would probably not need a highway or police department. The Towns could retain authority and responsibility for basic services.

Thus, the Peconic County movement comes again and again to the forefront of East End issues. Many see Peconic County as the framework to insure local control instead of being at the mercy of the western Suffolk. However, to make an informed decision about the future, East Enders will need detailed facts and the answer to many complex questions that will be raised pertaining to the formation of a new County.

The East End Mayors and Supervisors are in unanimous support of a financial feasibility study to assess the financial issues relevant to forming a new county. It is estimated that $100,000 would be needed to commission such a study. Specifically, the East End Towns and Villages request a grant of $50,000 from New York State to be matched with $50,000 from the local municipalities. It is recognized that the state performed a financial feasibility study pursuant to the proposed secession of Staten Island from New York City. As such, the East End towns seek assistance from the state to enable the residents to evaluate and assess the concept of Peconic County.

Proposed Action by the Governor:

THE GOVERNOR SHOULD propose legislation to provide $50,000 in funds to be matched by the by the East End Towns for the purpose of completing a feasibility study to assess the financial issues relevant to forming a new county.

BIOGRAPHIES OF GOVERNOR'S APPOINTEES

Kip Bedell

KIP BEDELL, a Long Island native, has been co-owner and winemaker at Bedell Cellars in Cutchogue since 1980. From 1970-90, he was the owner and president of Nassau Mutual Fuel Company. Bedell Cellars has received recognition from the wine industry, including being named 1990 New York Winery of the Year by the Beverage Tasting Institute. Mr. Bedell received a B.B.A. from George Washington University.

Betty Brown

BETTY BROWN lives with her family in the Town of Riverhead, and owns and operates a vegetable and fruit farm as well as the last remaining dairy farm on Long Island. She presently sits on the Board of Directors of The North Fork Environmental Council, a non-profit environmental organization serving the North Fork, and has served as a past president of that organization. She has been active on Suffolk County's Brown Tide Task Force since 1986. In the past, she has served on the Riverhead Town Agricultural Task Force and she is presently working on the Aquebogue and Jamesport Hamlet Task Forces. She is on the Board of Directors of Save The Bay, Inc. and is an active member of the Long Island Farm Bureau and the Jamesport, Aquebogue and Laurel Business Association. She co-chairs Riverhead Townscape, Inc. and has been appointed to chair the Riverhead Town Conservation Advisory Council.

Tony Bullock

TONY BULLOCK is a resident of Amagansett who was elected East Hampton Town Supervisor in 1987 and has since been re-elected three times. He is a former Town Councilman and Suffolk County Legislator. He graduated *cum laude* from Yale University with a B.A. in 1981. Supervisor Bullock was a prime sponsor of Suffolk County's land acquisition programs and developed and implemented East Hampton's solid waste management program. Supervisor Bullock serves as the Town's chief fiscal officer and is presently Chairman of the Suffolk County Supervisors' Association.

Larry Cantwell

LARRY CANTWELL is the Village Administrator in East Hampton Village and is the Governor's appointee to The Atlantic States Marine Fisheries Commission, one of three Commissioners from New York State. Between 1976 and 1983, he was an elected official in the Town of East Hampton serving for one year as Bay Constable and the remainder as a Town Councilman. Mr. Cantwell is a life-long resident of East Hapmton, a graduate of C.W. Post College, and has been an advocate of fisheries issues for over twenty years.

Rowland Vaughn Clark

ROWLAND CLARK, a third-generation waterman on Shelter Island, can trace fishing/whaling "roots" to pre-Revolutionary War times. He has worked on or about boats and water since childhood, serving in various capacities on commercial, sporting, pleasure and government craft. He was appointed this year to the U.S. Department of Commerce Marine Fisheries Advisory Committee and, in 1992, served on the Shellfish Advisory Committee, Waterways Advisory Committee and the Natural Resources Committee for the Town of Shelter Island. He has also chaired the Environmental Committee and acted as spokesperson at New York State Open Space hearings on behalf of the Shelter Island Association. Mr. Clark served as Councilman on the Shelter Island Town Board from 1984 to 1988, in addition to being a past member of the Montauk Boatmen's Association.

Sara Davison

SARA DAVISON, a resident of East Hampton, serves as Executive Director of both the Long Island and South Fork/Shelter Island Chapters of The Nature Conservancy. She holds a Bachelor of Science degree from Tulane University and a Master of Science degree in Botany and Ecology from Rutgers University. Prior to her current position, she served as the Conservancy's Director of Science and Stewardship for both the Pennsylvania and New Jersey programs. She has authored and co-authored a number of articles published in scientific journals and books.

Roberta Gosman Donovan

MS. DONOVAN, a resident of Montauk, was born in Amagansett. She attended the local schools as well as Rosemont College in Pennsylvania and the

University of Fribourg in Switzerland. Ms. Gosman is one of the owners and developers of Gosman's Dock and manages Gosman's Dock Restaurant. Gosman's Dock is a family-owned and -managed multiple business complex comprised of restaurants, a commercial dock and shoreside facility for commercial fishermen, several resort retail stores, and a wholesale-retail lobster and seafood business. Ms. Gosman served five years as Chairperson of the Montauk Citizens Advisory Committee, has served on the East Hampton Town Zoning Board of Appeals, and is currently a member of the East Hampton Town Planning Board. She is also a Trustee of The Nature Conservancy, a member of the Montauk Harbor Association, and a founding supporter of Music for Montauk.

Bran Ferren

BRAN FERREN, a resident of East Hampton, is a nationally recognized award-winning designer/technologist working in theater, film, music, product design, architecture and the sciences. In 1993, he joined Walt Disney Imagineering in the new position of Senior Vice President, Creative Technology. Prior to his current position, Ferren served as a consultant to Walt Disney Imagineering while heading his own firm. Associates & Ferren, a company established in 1978 in East Hampton, specializes in research and development, creative design, engineering and execution of projects and systems for the visual and performing arts as well as for industry and the sciences. Ferren has won numerous awards for his work, including the New York Drama Desk Award, the Los Angeles Critics' Circle Award and several awards from the Academy of Motion Picture Arts and Sciences.

Brenda A. Filmanski

BRENDA A. FILMANSKI, AICP, holds an M.A. in Political Science from the State University of New York at Stony Brook and a B.F.A., *cum laude*, from Syracuse University. She has been engaged in municipal planning for the Town of Riverhead since 1986. She is a member of the American Institute of Certified Planners, the American Planning Association, the National Trust for Historic Preservation, Hallockville, Inc., Riverhead Townscape, and served as Secretary of the Riverhead Bicentennial Commission (1991-92). She is a Riverhead resident and native.

Clifford H. Foster

CLIFFORD H. FOSTER, a third-generation farmer, resides with his family in Sagaponack and farms lands owned by his family as well as others in the area. He is presently a member of the Bridgehampton Board of Fire Commissioners and is on the VEEB Board for the Suffolk County Fire Training Center. In the past, Mr. Foster has served as President of the Long Island Farm Bureau and as a member of New York Farm Bureau Board of Directors.

Katherine McLane Francis

A TWELFTH-GENERATION resident of Water Mill, Ms. Francis is a Senior Vice-President of The Bank of the Hamptons, N.A. She holds a graduate degree from the Stonier Graduate School of Banking at the University of Delaware and a B.S. degree from Long Island University. In addition to being a member of the Kiwanis Club of Southampton and Zonta of Eastern Suffolk, she is active in many other community organizations. In 1992, Ms. Francis received a Distinguished Alumna Award from Long Island University. She was named "Woman of the Year" by the East End Women's Network in 1989 and has been honored by the Suffolk County Human Rights Commission for her efforts on behalf of women in the field of business.

Joseph H. Gergela, III

JOE GERGELA serves as Executive Director of the Long Island Farm Bureau, a membership organization of over 3,500 farmers, fishermen, agribusinessmen and individuals interested in a rural quality of life. As Executive Director, Mr. Gergela represents the interests of Long Island's agricultural industries before local, state and federal governments. Mr. Gergela is the former Suffolk County Executive Director of USDA Agricultural Stabilization and Conservation Service and working partner of Gergela Farms. He serves as President of the Riverhead Chamber of Commerce, is an executive board member of the Eastern Long Island Executive's Association, and a board member of the Long Island Partnership and Economic Roundtable. Mr. Gergela, a graduate of SUNY at Stony Brook, resides in Center Moriches with his family.

Carol Gristina

CAROL GRISTINA is an owner of Gristina Vineyards in Cutchogue which was established in 1983. She received a B.A. degree from Barnard College,

Columbia University. Long active in public and private higher education, she serves as a College Council member of the State University of New York. She studied food and wine in Italy, France and the United States and taught for a number of years before devoting all her time and energy to Gristina Vineyards, a critically acclaimed premier winery on the North Fork.

Peter L. Hallock

MR. HALLOCK is President and managing partner of Allan M. Schneider Associates, Inc., the largest real estate company on the East End, with offices in Southampton, Bridgehampton, East Hampton, Sag Harbor and Amagansett. Born and raised in Southampton, Peter was educated in the local school system and holds a Bachelors Degree from Boston University. Peter's heritage is steeped in the history of eastern Long Island, as he is a direct descendant of Peter Hallock, who first arrived at what is now Orient Point in the early 1600's. Peter is active in many local, civic and charitable organizations in the area.

Louisa Hargrave

LOUISA HARGRAVE was educated at Smith College, Harvard University and Simmons College. In 1973, Louisa and her husband, Alex, started the first commercial vineyard for wine grapes (*vitis vinifara*) on Long Island since 1750. Their 84-acre farm produces 10,000 cases of premium wine annually. Besides being winemaker at Hargrave Vineyards, Louisa is a director of Les Dames d'Escoffier, New York and a Trustee of The Old House in Cutchogue. She is a former director of the Cutchogue Library and the League of Women Voters of Riverhead-Southold.

Scott L. Harris

SCOTT HARRIS has served as Supervisor of the Town of Southold since 1990. His prior experience includes that of Southold Town Assessor, Suffolk County Legislative Administrative Aid and Southold Town Trustee. He is a member of the Suffolk County Supervisors' Association, serving as its Chairman in 1992, and the East End Supervisors' & Mayors' Association. Mr. Harris also serves on the New York State Association of Towns' Solid Waste Committee and the Peconic Bay Natural Estuary Management Committee. He is a member and past director of the Southold Town Baymen's Association and Ducks Unlimited. Mr. Harris holds a B.A. from Arizona State University.

Robert J. Hartmann

MR. HARTMANN was born into a farming family in St. James where he lived for many years before moving to Riverhead in the 1960's. He is the President of John A. Hartmann & Sons, Inc. which currently owns 300 acres, and has farmed as much as 400 acres. Mr. Hartmann is a past board member of the Long Island Farm Bureau and past director of the Empire State Potato Club. He also served as a volunteer fireman in St. James for many years. Currently, Mr. Hartmann is President of the St. James Sportsmen Club and is a board member of the Suffolk County Vocational and Extension Board and a member of the Dean's Council of the University Hospital at Stony Brook.

Curtis Highsmith

CURTIS HIGHSMITH is co-owner of B & C Cosmetics/Beauty Supplies based in Riverhead and leader/vocalist of the popular band, "The Reflections." Curtis currently serves on the Board of Directors of a number of civic organizations, including the Riverhead Chamber of Commerce, Community Awareness Program and Central Suffolk Hospital. He also serves on the Board of the Small Business Advisory Council for Suffolk County Executive Robert Gaffney. Curtis resides in Riverhead with his family.

Helen Hillman

HELEN HILLMAN is a real estate broker in East Hampton Town and has worked for The Condie Lamb Agency since 1973. An active member of the community, Helen sits on the Board of Directors of the East Hampton Day Care Center and previously spent six years as a member of the East Hampton School Board. She is currently a member of the East Hampton Town Anti-Bias Task Force. Helen resides in East Hapmton.

Joseph Janoski

JOE JANOSKI has served as Riverhead Town Supervisor since 1980. He is a graduate of Wilkes College and the University of Pennsylvania. Supervisor Janoski has served as Chairman of both the Suffolk County Supervisors' Association and the East End Supervisors' and Mayors' Association. He has served on the Suffolk County Executive's Transition Team, Suffolk County Charter Revision Commission, Highway Safety Task Force, Education Task Force, Long Island Regional Ashfill Board, and the Pine Barrens Advisory

Commission. He is a member of numerous fraternal organizations including the Knights of Columbus, American Military Retirees Association, Riverhead League of Women Voters, Hallockville, Inc., and the Air Force Association. He has been recognized on many occasions for outstanding achievement including two fellowships from the New York State Congress of Parents and Teachers and Man of the Year honors from the Riverhead Chamber of Commerce.

John Adam Kanas

JOHN KANAS serves as President and CEO of North Fork Bancorporation, the largest independent bank holding company in New York State. Mr. Kanas has been affiliated with numerous professional organizations, including past President of Long Island Bankers Association and past President of Independent Bankers Assocation of New York as well as New York State Bankers Legislative Policy Committee. Mr. Kanas was appointed by Governor Cuomo to serve on the Long Island Power Authority. He is a member of the President's Council of Southampton College and previously served on the Board of Trustees of Long Island University. Mr. Kanas holds a Bachelors degree from Southampton College and a Masters degree in Business Administration from C.W. Post College. He resides with his family in East Moriches.

Robert G. Kassner

BOB KASSNER, a resident of Southold, is the Site Plan Reviewer for the Town of Southold and a Civil Service qualified Planner. He graduated from New York University with a degree in management and marketing. Affiliations include the Long Island Chapter of the New York State Archaeological Association, New York Genealogical and Biographical Association, Certified Genealogical Record Searcher, Board for Certification, Washington, D.C., Southold Historical Society and Friends for Long Island Heritage.

Sharon Kast

SHARON KAST, a resident of Shelter Island, was recently elected as Councilman to the Shelter Island Town Board. Ms. Kast is a graduate of the University of Massachusetts and holder of a Certificate of Environmental Sciences from Long Island University. She served as Vice-President of Design and Merchandising for Murjani International (Gloria Vanderbilt) before moving to the Island. Ms. Kast is currently Chair of The Nature Conservancy's Mashomack Preserve Advisory Board and sits on the CAC of the Peconic Bay National Estuary Program. She also is a Trustee of the Shelter Island Association. Her government service includes chairing the Shelter Island Town Conservation Advisory Council and being a member of the Comprehensive Planning Committee. She also sits on the Suffolk County Council on Environmental Quality and the Suffolk County Solar Energy Commission.

Nancy Nagle Kelley

NANCY NAGLE KELLEY serves as Associate Director for Development and Government Relations for Guild Hall, the East End's primary cultural institution. Her prior experience includes Executive Director of the Suffolk Community College Foundation and President of Group for the South Fork. Ms. Kelley, a member of the American Institute of Certified Planners, has served on the Suffolk County Pine Barrens Commission and the Suffolk County Planning Commission, acting as Vice Chairman from 1990 to 1992. She has been appointed to numerous committees, incuding the Governor's Task Force on Coastal Resources and the New York State Tidal Wetlands Committee. Ms. Kelley was awarded the Annual Environmental Quality Award by the EPA. She currently sits on the Board of Directors of the Group for the South Fork and the East Hampton Youth Alliance. Ms. Kelley holds a Bachelors degree from Cornell University and a Masters degree from the John F. Kennedy School of Government at Harvard University. She resides with her family in Springs, East Hampton.

Steve Kenny

STEVE KENNY serves as Chairman of the Southampton Town Planning Board and is a Professor of Economics at Suffolk Community College in Riverhead, where he formally served as Executive Dean. His civic involvement includes having served as President of the Board of Directors of Cornell Cooperative Extension of Suffolk and trustee of the following organizations: Riverhead Chamber of Commerce, Central Suffolk Hospital, Long Island Nature Conservancy, New York State Nature Conservancy, and the East End Arts Council. In Southampton, Steve has also been a member of the Town's citizens advisory committees for open space and historic preservation. He lives in Remsenbrg with his family.

Lisa Liquori

LISA LIQUORI, a resident of Amagansett, has served as the Planning Director for the Town of East Hampton since 1986. Ms. Liquori earned a Masters of Regional Planning Degree from the University of Pennsylvania. As Planning Director, Ms. Liquori has developed, implemented and obtained over $2.5 million in state and federal grants for the preservation and the promotion of open space, farmland, environmental resources, fisheries, affordable housing, and historic preservation. She is currently serving as the Technical Advisory Chairwoman to the Peconic Estuary Program and is preparing the Town's Waterfront Revitalization Program.

Richard Lofstad, Jr.

MR. LOFSTAD, a third-generation East End fishermen, resides with his family in East Quogue. While attending Florida Junior College in Jacksonville, he worked for a company which sold fish nationally and internationally. After captaining a boat for three years, he founded the Shinnecock Fishermen's Cooperative, the only such cooperative in New York State. Having worked as a manger of a seafood company for the past three years, Mr. Lofstad recently formed his own seafood export business, Long Island Seafood Export, Inc. He is one of the commercial representatives serving on the Marine Resource Advisory Council of the New York State Department of Environmental Conservation. He is also on the board of directors of Seafood Harvesters Association of New York as well as the New York Seafood Promotion Council.

Joseph J. McBride

JOSEPH J. MCBRIDE is a charter boat captain and a resident of East Hampton, and has been president of the Montauk Boatmen and Captains' Association for the past 15 years. Mr. McBride is a retired New York City School Administrator and has operated a charter boat for the past 15 years out of Montauk. He has served on the National Marine Fisheries Sportsfishing Advisory Board and the Blue Fish and Shark Plan Advisory Boards.

Kevin McDonald

KEVIN MCDONALD is Vice-President of Group for the South Fork, a not-for-profit environmental organization serving the Towns of East Hampton, Southampton and Shelter Island. In his 11 years at the Group, he has assisted in drafting legislation to better protect the natural resources of the East End at the Town, County and State levels. He has been a major player in both the inclusion of the Peconic Bays into the National Estuary Program and 1993's important legislation to protect the Pine Barrens of Long Island. Mr. McDonald's participation on committees and boards includes: Chairman of Citizens Advisory Committee, National Estuary Program, Southampton Town Agriculture Advisory Committee, Governor Cuomo's Task Force on Coastal Resources, New York State Tidal Wetlands Advisory Committee, and Save the Peconic Bays. Mr. McDonald earned a B.S. degree from St. John's University and has earned graduate credits toward his M.A. at Stony Brook University. He resides with his family in Hampton Bays.

Edward J. Merz

EDWARD J. MERZ, a resident of Jamesport, has served as Chief Executive Officer of Suffolk County National Bank since 1987. He is a graduate of City University of New York and Rutgers University. He is a past president of the Long Island Division of the New York State Bankers Association, the Long Island Bankers Association, the Riverhead Rotary Cub and, most recently, the Independent Bankers Association of New York State. Currently, Ed is a director of the Independent Bankers of America and represents New York State. He has served as an officer of Central Suffolk Hospital, Suffolk County Boy Scouts, Industrial Development Agency of Riverhead, and the Riverhead Chamber of Commerce.

Peter J. Needham

PETER NEEDHAM, a Shelter Island resident of twenty years, is the owner and operator of Coecles Harbor Marina and Boatyard on the Island. He is a member of the Board of Directors of the Association of Marine Industries, previously serving as President and Vice-President. Mr. Needham serves on numerous committees and associations, including the New York Sea Grant Extension Marine Facilities Program Advisory Committee, EPA's Peconic Estuary Program, EPA's Long Island Sound Study, Long Island Pine Barrens Maritime Reserve Council and the American Boatbuilders & Repairers Association. Mr. Needham holds a Bachelors degree in marine science from Long Island University.

Robert J. Palmer

ROBERT PALMER is the owner of Palmer Vineyards on Long Island's North Fork. In addition, he is President and Chief Executive Officer of R.J. Palmer, Inc., a $100 million media negotiating service in Manhattan. Prior to these endeavors, he was President and Chief Executive Officer of Kelly, Nason/Univas, the U.S. partner of a world-wide advertising consortium.

Sherry Patterson

SHERRY PATTERSON, who resides with her faimly in Riverhead, served on the Riverhead Zoning Board of Appeals from 1982 to 1986 and chaired the Riverhead Affordable Housing Task Force. She is a member of the Riverhead Chamber of Commerce and a Trustee of the Riverhead Free Library. A graduate of the American Real Estate School, she is currently employed by Edwin Fishel Tuccio Real Estate in Riverhead.

Mary Bess Phillips

MARY BESS PHILLIPS is co-owner with her husband of the *F/V Illusion*, a commercial fishing vessel. In addition to her commercial fishery business, she is active with the following organizations: Board of Directors of the New York Seafood Council; director and founding member of the Seafood Harvesters Association of New York; director and founding member of the East Coast Fisheries Foundation; Cornell Cooperative Extension Advisory Committee for the Marine Program; and appointed member of the Historic Review Commission for the Village of Greenport. Mary Bess resides in Greenport with her family.

Paul F. Rickenbach, Jr.

PAUL F. RICKENBACH, JR. is Mayor of the Village of East Hampton, having been elected in 1992 after serving as Village Trustee for four years. Mayor Rickenbach is a former police officer with the Village of East Hampton and retired from the position of detective after serving for twenty years. Mayor Rickenbach was chosen by the East End Mayors to represent them on the Governor's East End Economic and Environmental Task Force.

William J. Sanok

WILLIAM J. SANOK resides in Mattituck and is employed as an Agricultural Program Leader by the Cornell Cooperative Extension of Suffolk County. He received his B.S. degree from Cornell University and an M.S. degree from Michigan State University. Over the past 26 years, he has worked with the potato and vegetable industries on Long Island, and from 1973 through 1986, also worked very closely with the developing Long Island grape and wine industries. More recently, his major responsibilities have been in the area of land use, farmland preservation, food issues and food safety. As Agricultural Program Leader, he supervises a staff of seven agricultural agents working with the agricultural and horticultural interests in Suffolk County, the leading agricultural county in New York State.

John H. Scheetz

JOHN SCHEETZ, who resides in Westhampton, is currently president and chief executive officer of Pride Guides, Inc., a publishing firm engaged in publishing tourist guides and related tourist material. He has a broad background in tourism, having served on the Board of Directors of the Long Island Tourist and Convention Commission and as president of the Greater Westhampton Chamber of Commerce. He is currently Chairman of the South Fork Promotion Committee and a member of the Pine Barrens Advisory Committee. He formerly published a weekly newspaper in Brookhaven Town and served as Executive Secretary of the Suffolk County Water Authority for 21 years.

John Scotti

JOHN SCOTTI has had sixteen years of experience with Cornell Cooperative Extension Association of Suffolk County and the New York Sea Grant Extension Program. His present position is that of Marine Program Leader and Acting Farm Program Leader for the Suffolk County Farm & Education Center. He is a member of the Board of Directors of the Long Island Farm Bureau, *ex officio* member of the New York Seafood Council, Shinnecock Fishermen's Cooperative, Inlet Seafood Corporation and is a member of Epsilon Sigma Phi, Lambda Chapter, Cornell University. Mr. Scotti lives in Riverhead.

Huson Sherman

HOOT SHERMAN, Supervisor of the Town of Shelter Island since 1992, was raised on the Island and graduated from the local high school. He is a graduate of Florida State University and served for 21 years in the Navy. In 1981, he was awarded the Navy's Meritorious Service Medal and retired at the rank of Commander. Past and current civic involvement includes: President and Secretary of the Shelter Island Lions, Treasurer of the American Legion, member of the Shelter Island Heights Volunteer Fire Department, and co-founder and member of the Board of Directors of the Shelter Island Youth Center.

Fred W. Thiele, Jr.

FRED W. THIELE, JR. has been Supervisor of the Town of Southampton since 1992 and is a life-long resident of Sag Harbor. Mr. Thiele is a graduate of Southampton College of Long Island University and received his law degree from Albany Law School. He was the Southampton Town Attorney from 1982-87 and East Hampton Planning Board Attorney from 1982-86. Mr. Thiele served as a Suffolk County Legislator for the 16th District, which is comprised of the Towns of Southampton, East Hampton, Shelter Island and a portion of Brookhaven Town and served as the Chairman of the Legislature's Energy and Environment Committee.

Thomas J. Tobin

THOMAS TOBIN is President and Chief Executive Officer of The Bridgehampton National Bank which operates six local offices in the communities of Bridgehampton, East Hampton, Mattituck, Southampton and Southold. He has been a member of the banking community on the East End for over 25 years and President of Bridgehampton National Bank since 1986. Mr. Tobin is a former instructor with the American Institute of Banking's Eastern Suffolk Chapter and has been affiliated with The Peconic Land Trust. He resides in Southampton with his famiy.

Thomas A. Twomey, Jr.

TOM TWOMEY, a resident of East Hampton, is the founding partner of Twomey, Latham, Shea & Kelley, one of the largest law firms in Suffolk County. He has been practicing law on the East End since 1973. Mr. Twomey is a Trustee of the Long Island Power Authority appointed by the Governor in 1989. Prior to that, he was appointed by the Governor to the New York State Freshwater Wetlands Appeals Board in 1979 and to the New York State Energy Council in 1978. He has served as an Assistant Town Attorney and as Special Counsel to the Zoning Board of Appeals for the Town of Southampton. He has served as a Special Assistant District Attorney for Suffolk County. Tom is a member of the Board of Directors of Guild Hall, the art and cultural center of East Hampton. He also serves as a member of the Dean's Council of the University Hospital at Stony Brook and is a member of the East Hampton Library Expansion Committee. Mr. Twomey has been awarded Martindale-Hubbell's highest rating for legal competence and professional reliability and is in "Who's Who in American Law." He received his Bachelor of Arts from Manhattan College, attended the University of Virginia Law School, and received his Juris Doctor from Columbia Law School in 1970.

Lyle C. Wells

LYLE WELLS' family has been farming on the East End of Long Island since the 1600's. He has operated his family's farm in Riverhead since 1981. He has an Associates degree in Business Administration from the New York State School in Delhi. He is a past President of the Long Island Farm Bureau and has served on its various committees as well as those of the Cornell Cooperative Extension. He is currently on the Board of Directors of the New York State Vegetable Growers. Mr. Wells currently farms approximately 100 acres.

Jack Van de Wetering

JACK VAN DE WETERING is President of Ivy Acres, a multi-million-dollar greenhouse operation. He was born in Holland and came to the United States with his family at the age of 11. Today, Ivy Acres encompasses 20 acres. Fifty million plants are grown each season and shipped to garden centers from Boston to Washington, D.C. Jack is active in many business and community organizations including the Professional Plant Growers Association. He has been a Rotarian since 1973 and a vital member of the Riverhead Townscape Committee. He resides in Calverton.

Raymond G. Wesnofske

RAY WESNOFSKE has resided in Bridgehampton since 1954 when his family moved there to continue their farming operation. He attended Bridgehampton High School and Cornell University's Agricultural School. He started his own potato farming and packaging business in Bridgehampton and subsequently acquired a working 500-acre potato farm in Florida. In addition to his farming business, he has invested in a number of commercial real estate ventures. He joined the board of the Bridgehampton National Bank in 1970 and has served as its Chairman since 1989. He also serves on the Southampton Town Agricultural Advisory Committee.

Thomas F. Whelan

THOMAS WHELAN is an attorney with the firm of Esseks, Hefter & Angel in Riverhead. He previously served as Babylon Town Attorney and as principal law secretary to a Supreme Court and County Court Judge. Mr. Whelan is a graduate of Columbia University and Brooklyn Law School. He resides with his wife in the Riverhead hamlet of Wading River.

Alice Wise

ALICE WISE is employed by Cornell Cooperative Extension of Suffolk County as the Viticultural Research Specialist, based at the Long Island Horticultural Research Lab in Riverhead. As viticultural researcher, she conducts applied research and coordinates educational programs for the Long Island wine industry. Ms. Wise received a B.S. in Horticulture in 1983 from the University of Maryland and an M.S. in Pomology in 1987 from Cornell University. She is a professional member of the American Society for Enology and Viticulture. She resides on the North Fork with her husband.

APPENDICES

APPENDIX A

IN SENATE
S. 4654

STATE OF NEW YORK

4654
1993-1994 Regular Sessions
IN SENATE
April 27, 1993

Introduced by Sens. KUHL, COOK, HOLLAND, LARKIN, MARCHI, SALAND, SEARS, SEWARD, WRIGHT—read twice and ordered printed, and when printed to be committed to the Committee on Agriculture

AN ACT to amend the agriculture and markets law, in relation to agricultural assessments

THE PEOPLE OF THE STATE OF NEW YORK, REPRESENTED IN SENATE AND ASSEMBLY, DO ENACT AS FOLLOWS:

Section 1. Subdivision 4 of section 301 of the agriculture and markets law is amended by adding a new paragraph f to read as follows:

F. LAND OF NOT LESS THAN TEN ACRES USED AS A SINGLE OPERATION IN THE PRECEDING TWO YEARS FOR THE PRODUCTION FOR SALE OF CROPS, LIVESTOCK OR LIVESTOCK PRODUCTS OF AN AVERAGE GROSS SALES VALUE OF TEN THOUSAND DOLLARS OR MORE, OR LAND OF LESS THAN TEN ACRES USED AS A SINGLE OPERATION IN THE PRECEDING TWO YEARS FOR THE PRODUCTION FOR SALE OF CROPS, LIVESTOCK OR LIVESTOCK PRODUCTS OF AN AVERAGE GROSS SALES VALUE OF FIFTY THOUSAND DOLLARS OR MORE.

S 2. This act shall take effect immediately.

IN ASSEMBLY
s. 4806

STATE OF NEW YORK

4806

1993-1994 Regular Sessions
IN ASSEMBLY
March 2, 1993

Introduced by M. of A. PARMENT—Multi-Sponsored by—M. of A. MCENENY—read once and referred to the Committee on Agriculture

AN ACT to amend the agriculture and markets law, in relation to the definition of land used in agricultural production

THE PEOPLE OF THE STATE OF NEW YORK, REPRESENTED IN SENATE AND ASSEMBLY, DO ENACT AS FOLLOWS:

Section 1. The opening paragraph of subdivision 4 of section 301 of the agriculture and markets law, as separately amended by chapters 316 and 797 of the laws of 1992, is amended to read as follows:

"Land used in agricultural production" means not less than ten acres of land used as a single operation in the preceding two years for the production for sale of crops, livestock or livestock products of an average gross sales value of ten thousand dollars or more; OR, NOT LESS THAN TEN ACRES OF LAND USED IN THE PRECEDING TWO YEARS TO SUPPORT A COMMERCIAL HORSE BOARDING OPERATION WITH ANNUAL GROSS RECEIPTS OF TEN THOUSAND DOLLARS OR MORE. Land used in agricultural production shall not include land or portions thereof used for processing or retail merchandising of such crops, livestock or livestock products. Land used in agricultural production shall also include:

S 2. Section 301 of the agriculture and markets law is amended by adding a new subdivision 13 to read as follows:

13. "COMMERCIAL HORSE BOARDING OPERATION" MEANS AN AGRICULTURAL ENTERPRISE, CONSISTING OF AT LEAST TEN ACRES AND HAVING AT ALL TIMES AT LEAST TEN HORSES, THAT RECEIVES TEN THOUSAND DOLLARS OR MORE IN GROSS RECEIPTS ANNUALLY FROM FEES GENERATED EITHER THROUGH THE BOARDING OF HORSES OR THROUGH THE PRODUCTION AND SALE OF CROPS, LIVESTOCK, AND LIVESTOCK PRODUCTS, OR THROUGH BOTH SUCH BOARDING AND SUCH PRODUCTION.

S 3. This act shall take effect July 1, 1993 and shall apply to city and town assessment rolls completed subsequent to March 1, 1994 and to village assessment rolls completed subsequent to January 1, 1995.

FISHERIES LANDING STATISTICS FOR NEARBY STATES OF NEW YORK, NEW JERSEY, CONNECTICUT, RHODE ISLAND.
(IN THOUSANDS)

	1987	1988	1989	1990	1991	1992
RHODE ISLAND						
POUNDS	100,150	106,208	125,041	131,782	139,805	141,655
DOLLARS	$77,424	$69,422	$75,004	$72,889	$85,111	$85,681
NEW JERSEY						
POUNDS	116,141	112,617	128,459	149,369	175,841	204,368
DOLLARS	$72,643	$71,863	$78,802	$89,344	$96,865	$97,500
NEW YORK						
POUNDS	40,882	38,508	37,080	48,823	50,823	50,112
DOLLARS	$53,352	$54,224	$51,096	$56,474	$53,161	$53,985
CONNECTICUT						
POUNDS	8,562	9,133	8,588	9,471	14,905	19,634
DOLLARS	$15,974	$17,444	$18,309	$26,873	$44,815	$62,672

OUR LIVING OCEANS

THE FIRST ANNUAL REPORT ON THE STATUS OF U.S. LIVING MARINE RESOURCES

November 1991
NOAA Tech. Memo. NMFS-F/SPO-1

U.S. DEPARTMENT OF COMMERCE

Robert Mosbacher
Secretary

NATIONAL OCEANIC AND ATMOSPHERIC ADMINISTRATION

John A. Knauss
Under Secretary for Oceans and Atmosphere

NATIONAL MARINE FISHERIES SERVICE

William W. Fox, Jr.
Assistant Administrator for Fisheries

...Principal Groundfish and Flounders

stocks were the lowest ever recorded.

Groundfish partly recovered during the late 1970's because overall fishing efforts were reduced by restrictive management under the International Commission for the Northwest Atlantic Fisheries (ICNAF) and by the advent of the Magnuson Fishery Conservation and Management Act (MFCMA) in 1976. Cod and haddock numbers increased markedly; pollock and several flounder stocks also grew. Overall, the groundfish stock index peaked in 1978, then began to decline again and fell in 1987 and 1988 to extremely low values. The 1989 and 1990 index values were slightly higher than the previous two years, primarily owing to recruitment of moderate 1987 year classes of Atlantic cod and yellowtail flounder.

Domestic fishing for northeast demersal fishes increased rapidly after the MFCMA took effect in 1977 and more than doubled during the first 10 years. Effort has remained at near-peak levels, despite large declines in overall catch.

Skates and Dogfish Sharks

Dogfish and skates are a significant and growing part of overall northeast groundfish stocks (Fig. 1-2). Of the two dogfishes (spiny and smooth), the spiny dogfish is dominant by far. Seven species of skates (little, winter, barndoor, brier, thorny, leopard, and smooth-tailed) occur on the northeast shelf, but three (winter, little, and thorny skates) produce most of the landings.

Skate and spiny dogfish landings have increased in recent years (spiny dogfish landings in 1990 were 14,300 t, up from 4,500 t in 1989; total skate landings were 11,300 t in 1990, up from 6,600 t in 1989). Nevertheless, these landings levels remain well below the long-term potential landings and the current potential yields for these fish. This is due to a steady increase in the stocks throughout the 1970's and 1980's (Fig. 1-2). Survey catches of both dogfish and skates since 1986 have been the highest observed. These dogfish and skate increases, coupled with groundfish and flounder declines, indicate that the proportion of dogfish and skates in the Georges Bank surveys has risen from roughly 25% in 1963 to nearly 75% in recent years.

Figure 1-2.—U.S. commercial landings and abundance indices for skates and dogfish off the northeastern U.S. coast, 1960-90. Abundance indices are mean weight (kg) per tow taken in NEFSC spring bottom trawl surveys. Species include little, winter, barndoor, brier, thorny, leopard, smooth-tailed skates, and spiny and smooth dogfish.

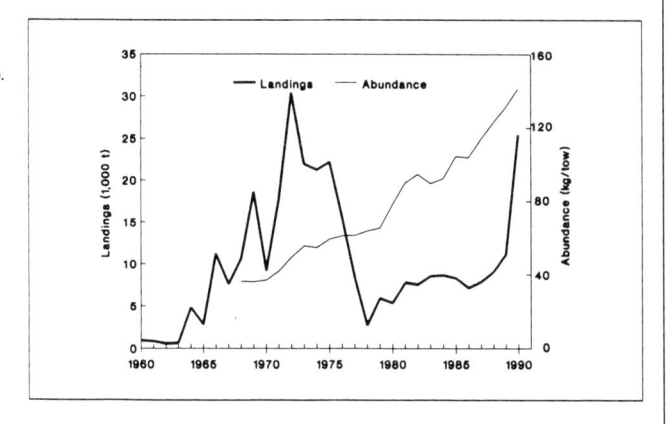

BROWN TIDE COMPREHENSIVE ASSESSMENT AND MANAGEMENT PROGRAM

SUMMARY

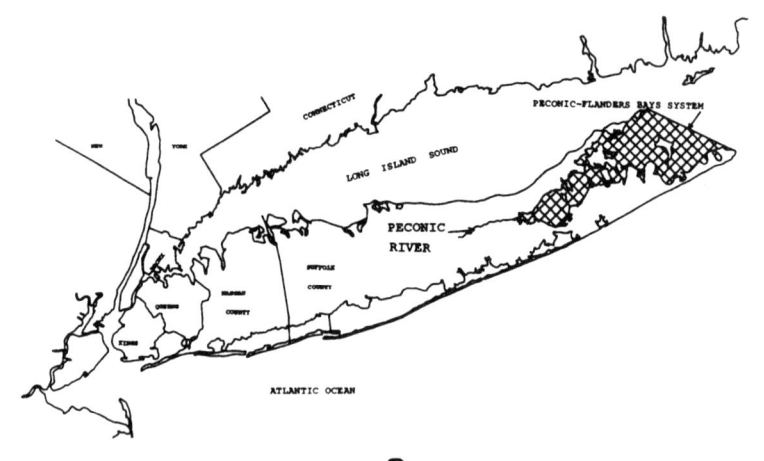

Robert J. Gaffney
County Executive

Mary E. Hibberd, M.D., M.P.H.
Commissioner

SUFFOLK COUNTY
DEPARTMENT OF HEALTH SERVICES

November, 1992

embayments, pollution sources and facilities such as Sag Harbor Village STP require additional evaluation to determine localized impacts and potential remedial measures.

4. Stormwater Runoff and Coliform Control

a) Stormwater runoff remediation efforts should be evaluated and undertaken on a site-specific basis pursuant to localized studies which demonstrate technological, economic, and environmental feasibility.

b) On a system-wide basis, any action which would result in a substantial increase in stormwater runoff coliform loading to the Peconic Estuary system should be strictly prohibited. Proposals for new development within the stormwater runoff-contributing area to the Peconic Estuary system should be reviewed under the strictest scrutiny. In addition to on-site stormwater runoff containment requirements, vegetative buffers and sediment and erosion control plans should be considered as part of the approval process, with enforcement through the issuance and revocation of permits.

5. Boating and Marina Controls

a) The Suffolk County law (Resolution #946-88) which mandates the SCDHS to undertake investigation of potential nuisances at marinas should be implemented in the Peconic Estuary system so that marine pollution data could be obtained; to date, this law has not been implemented due to SCDHS staffing limitations. These data could be utilized to specifically identify boating and marina problems and management needs and to conduct an informed evaluation of the feasibility of potential control alternatives. Until such an evaluation occurs, the highest possible standard of review for marina projects should be employed to assure minimal adverse environmental impacts from marina construction and operation.

b) Greater use of shore-based toilets, holding tanks on boats, and existing and additional pump-out stations should be promoted, especially in areas with heavy boat traffic or in environmentally sensitive areas. The implementation of other measures, such as designation of "no discharge zones" and enforcement for non-compliance with discharge regulations, may also increase usage of pump-out facilities.

6. Natural Resources

a) Restoration and monitoring of natural resources which have been adversely impacted by the Brown Tide should occur in conjunction with other pollution control measures outlined in this section. Examples of potential priority restoration and monitoring targets should be scallop reseeding and eelgrass replanting.

b) Water quality management decisions should be accompanied by the maximum practicable level of protection and enhancement of affected natural resources, based on a comprehensive analysis of available data and the selection of the most protective resource management alternative which is feasible from social, economic, and technological perspectives.

c) A Peconic Estuary-specific natural resource inventory and management plan should be pursued for the Peconic Estuary system. Several suggestions regarding management were made in the *Workshop for the Development of a Research Program for the Peconic Bay Responsive to Management Needs* report (MSRC et al, November, 1991) which points out that, from a natural resources perspective, management information for the

Voters Asked to Finance Bay Cleanup

By Barbara Goffman
STAFF WRITER

Southampton voters will be asked to decide Nov. 2 if cleaning up the Peconic and other local bays is worth a few dollars a year to them.

The town board yesterday voted to ask residents to approve selling $2 million worth of bonds to finance 34 storm-water abatement projects over the next two years.

The town probably could get a low interest rate for the bonds, less than 5 percent, Supervisor Fred Thiele said. Therefore, an owner of a $200,000 home for example, would pay at most an extra $3.60 a year in real property taxes to pay back the bond and its interest over the next 15 years, he said.

"This is an opportunity for taxpayers to get a big bang for their dollar," he said.

Currently runoff from all Southampton roads drain directly in the bays. So car oil and animal waste on the roads, as well as pesticides in roadside grass, get washed into the bays when it rains. The pollution has resulted in waters so unhealthy that many East End bays have been closed to harvesting shellfish and other crops.

If voters approve the bond sale, basins will be built under the sewers to catch the first half-inch of rain water, with which most ground pollutants mix. Water in the basins will drain back into the ground. The rest of the rain water, which is mainly clean, will continue to run into the bays, Thiele said.

"Water quality will improve immediately, within a few months," said Wayne Grothe, Southampton Town Baymen's Association secretary. With fewer pesticides in the bays, more animals could live, and, perhaps, shellfishing may come back within five years, he said.

"Storm water projects have worked elsewhere, such as Fish Cove near the North Sea area," Thiele said. "In the past three years, we have done four projects, including Fish Cove, through our operating budget. But it would take 15 years to do all 34 projects if we went through the operating budget."

And the town doesn't have 15 years, Grothe said.

"The longer you wait, the harder and more expensive it is to clean up," he said. "We have more waters closed to clamming than towns to the west of us. Around 45 percent of all waters around Southampton are closed in the summer. In 1982 there were approximately 300 full-time baymen in Southampton town. There are maybe 20 now."

The bays are so dirty that clams, scallops, oysters, fish and shellfish can't survive, Grothe said. "You're closer to closing some areas to swimming than opening them to shellfishing ... The pollution in the inland bays is so bad that baby fish don't survive. Most of them don't even hatch," he added.

Seventy to 90 percent of the bay pollution comes from contaminated rain water, he said.

Grothe is hopeful that cleaning the bays will help end brown tide, an algae that has plagued East End waters since 1985 and that basically has killed off the scallop crop. Thiele isn't as optimistic, but said, "The silver-lining of the Brown Tide problem is that its research found that storm-water runoff is the key problem of bay pollution."

Thirteen of the catch basins would be built under sewers that feed into the Peconic Bay. Other sewer basins would include: 10 that feed into the Shinnecock Bay, 3 that run into Mecox Bay and two that drain into Moriches Bay.

Thiele hopes that a Southampton commitment to cleaning the bays will attract federal and state funding for further efforts. He thinks the bond issue will pass.

"I know the bond issue has strong support from environmental groups and the Southampton Baymen's Association," he said.

Casting A Wider Net

BY WARREN STRUGATCH

When it comes to trading fish stories, Rick Lofstad doesn't want to tell about the one that got away. He doesn't even want to describe the one he landed.

The one he landed lives on dry land, walks, talks and, most importantly, imports. After an $83,000 market study and two trips to Europe, Lofstad finally landed the European customer that proved so elusive. Where in Europe? Western Europe, somewhere. That's as precise as Lofstad, a third-generation Montauk commercial fisherman, is willing to get.

Did you ever know a fisherman to broadcast where the fish were biting?

As both independent fisherman and packaging representative for 30 fellow East End commercial fishermen, Lofstad and his associate, Thomas Mahl, worked hard to reel in their first big European customer. Now Lofstad is packaging East End fish and shipping them by air to Europe, making one of Long Island's original products one of its newest exports.

Despite high costs for air freight, the exporting fishermen are lured by higher wholesale prices and a population that eats more fish more often than do most Americans.

State officials, who helped finance the European market study and subsequent trade missions, pronounce the project a success.

"Ricky is selling big over there, whether he chooses to talk about it or not," said Nancy Kunz, a Department of State employee based in Albany. As a specialist in commercial fisheries, she coordinated the trade missions.

Lofstad's reticence doesn't surprise Andrew Kaelin, a private consultant hired for the project. "You ask him how much he sells or where he sells it, he'll probably growl at you," said Kaelin, a former seafood exporter himself. "But I understand that. It's a competitive situation."

Efforts by the state to help East End fishermen sell overseas reflect growing government export assistance, on levels ranging from federal to county. Increasingly, exporters are seen as job producers. Financing export programs is even getting competitive. "New Jersey, for example, is helping its fishermen export, and they fish the same waters as ours do," Kunz said.

In New York, the state Department of Economic Development is financing export marketing efforts through a program called GEMS, or Global Export Market Studies.

Flat wholesale prices have prompted local fishermen to look beyond their traditional tristate market. While the lack of a convenient full-service processing plant hampers efforts to ship long distances by land, fishermen are realizing they can ship their catch overseas faster. It isn't easy, however. No fishermen can predict the amount of the landing, the species caught or exact time of return. They do know, however, that they had better get their product to market, and fast.

"How do you reserve air cargo space in advance, before you know what you're going to catch?" asked Lofstad, frustration in his voice. "How does the fisherman know what's swimming in the water, or what weather conditions will affect the landings? But if you want to ship, you obviously have to plan for transportation, and that means air freight."

Why bother? The answer is simple: economics.

"Wholesale prices haven't risen in 10 years," said John Scotti of the New York State Sea Grant program, part of the Cornell Cooperative Extension Service in Riverhead.

Prices for some species, like mackerel, have bottomed out at around 10 cents a pound. Yet mackerel is a Mediterranean favorite, and wholesalers there pay 10 to 15 times the U.S. rate. Skate, another fish popular in southern Europe and also caught off Montauk, brings higher prices, too, particularly in Spain.

To explore the European market, Lofstad received a $38,600 grant from the state, then raised more than $40,000 from local fishermen. The market knowledge gained would benefit Inlet Seafood Inc., which Lofstad represents on behalf of 10 boat-owning fishermen in Montauk and the 20 independent fishermen making up the Shinnecock Bay Cooperative and working with Inlet. The funds paid for Kaelin's market study and two follow-up trade missions.

Trade missions, a familiar market development tool to experienced exporters, proved less familiar on the East End docks. The co-ed character of this one prompted a good-ol-boys reaction that didn't surprise Lofstad. For all their hooting, however, the fishermen shared a sense of urgency. Said consultant Kaelin: "The whole point of the program was to get the business to diversify, to find new markets. In this case we were looking overseas, because Europeans and Asians consume five or six times more fish than we do."

Finn Anderson, who owns Erikson-Lindsen, a seafood export management company in Wantagh, said, "Long Island lobsters are selling big and so are dogfish. Whitefish goes as bait here, but gets 10 or 15 times as much in Europe, where it's eaten for dinner. Maybe 5 or 10 percent of the fish caught off the Sound end up exported."

The annual catch of Long Island commercial fishermen is about $50 million, according to government and private sources. That comprises almost all of New York State's commercial seafood business.

Japanese wholesalers, who began courting East Coast fishermen in the early 1980s, still represent an important, but demanding, seasonal market for fluke and tuna. Unlike most customers, who either accept or reject fish, the Japanese insist fish be caught the Japanese way. Throughout the '80s they trained thousands of American fishermen in the subtleties of catching fish for the sushi and sashimi markets.

"You've got to catch them the Japanese way, without the fish fighting back," Lofstad said. "They fight back, the flesh gets red with blood, and the sashimi market doesn't want it."

While Japanese customers are eagerly pursuing American fishermen, European markets are a tougher sell, especially with new European regulations coming into effect in January. The regulations, reflecting growing U.S.-European Community trade tensions, will impose inspection requirements that will effectively shut out American fishermen.

Indeed, trade tensions caused some uncomfortable moments on the New Yorkers' missions. In Madrid, Kunz recalled, "We were trying to talk business with these Spanish seafood guys, who are polite and everything, but something's bothering them. They come right out and tell you: 'I'd be happier buying from you if your government didn't keep Spanish boats from fishing your waters.'
"What can you do? You nod your head."

The next mission was planned for another big seafood country: Italy. This time, Mahl, Inlet's dock manager, made the trip with Kunz and Kaelin. By comparison, the Spanish trade mission was a roaring success. The Italians sniffed at Mahl's offer as if it had sat too long on the dock.

"The problem," Mahl said, "was that the Italian market would take frozen and we were offering fresh. There wasn't much at the present time we could do about that."

Lofstad wants that to change. "What we need is a processing plant near the docks where we can dry and pack fish. That's what the market wants. That's what I've been talking to people about." He's not specific on details, but sources say he has been pressing government and private interests to clear the way for construction of a processing plant.

Fellow exporter Anderson agrees that a large-scale local processing plant would open new markets. "Cryogenic freezing improves the taste in most cases since it prevents spoilage, and obviously makes transportation easier," he said. But building a new plant involves cooperation between fishermen accustomed to competition.

"These guys are fiercely independent and aren't used to working together to bring about change," Anderson said. "They're short on capital now because of last winter's storms. What they need is a Billy Joel to speak for them, like the baymen have. Maybe a Christie Brinkley."

Warren Strugatch is a free-lance writer.

Fish Tales

The Long Island offshore fishing industry, which accounts for the overwhelming share of the commercial catch in New York State, can spin some sad fish stories. Although the state catch has increased by one-third in the past five years, the total revenue to commercial fishermen has been flat.

	Pounds bought by wholesalers (in millions)	Landing price paid to fishermen (in millions)
1982	35.778	$45.4
1983	38.187	38.5
1984	38.902	39.9
1985	39.233	38.0
1986	43.628	45.5
1987	40.882	53.4
1988	38.508	54.2
1989	37.080	51.1
1990	48.823	56.5
1991	50.823	53.2
1992	50.112	54.0

SOURCE: National Marine Fisheries Service, U.S. Dept. of Commerce

APPENDIX H 183

MARIO M. CUOMO
GOVERNOR

STATE OF NEW YORK
EXECUTIVE DEPARTMENT
OFFICE OF GENERAL SERVICES
MAYOR ERASTUS CORNING 2ND TOWER
THE GOVERNOR NELSON A. ROCKEFELLER EMPIRE STATE PLAZA
ALBANY, N.Y. 12242

ROBERT B. ADAMS
COMMISSIONER

September 13, 1993

Mr. Larry Cantwell
Village Administrator
Village of East Hampton
27 Main St.,
East Hampton, NY 11937

Dear Mr. Cantwell:

As you requested, I am enclosing a report which indicates sales of fish products from the Office of General Services, Division of Supply Support to the various State facilities which we serve. These figures represent sales for the State Fiscal Year ending March 31, 1993.

If you have any questions, please feel free to call me at (518) 474-6789.

Sincerely,

Richard C. Fanch
Director,
Division of Supply Support

RF:jh
Enclosure

"OGS ... COMMITTED TO TOTAL CUSTOMER SATISFACTION"

recycled paper

Office of General Services
DIVISION OF SUPPLY SUPPORT

SALES OF FISH PRODUCTS
1992-1993

No.	Commodity — Description		Quantity Sold Cases	Pounds	Sales Value
0170220	FISH STICKS FROZ 1OZ	60LB	6,488	389,280	559,456
0170330	FISH, GEFILTE	6/10	629	24,908	14,104
0170732	FISH, TUNA CHUNK 4.2LB	6/CS	17,831	449,341	536,463
0170738	FISH, TUNA CHK 4.2LB SL	6/CS	165	4,125	170
0171321	FISH, FRIED PORT 2-2/3 OZ	60LB	10,394	623,640	945,546
0171420	FISH, RAW PORT FRZ 3 OZ	60LB	2,802	168,120	232,141
0171430	FISH, POLLOCK, RAWTAIL 4OZ	36#	1,592	57,312	68,001
0171820	FISH COD PORT 2OZ 4LB	24LB	8,645	207,480	225,464
0171821	COD FISH PORT 2OZ FRO5LB006/CS		34	1,020	1,033
0171822	FISH COD PORT 2OZ 4.5LB	27LB	36	972	1,203
0171824	FISH, COD, RAW PORT 4OZ FR36LBCS		372	13,392	21,598
0171825	FISH, COD, RAW PORT 4OZ FR	60LB	1,452	87,120	195,166
0171845	FISH, POLLOCK, BRDD FILET	4OZ36#	4,133	148,788	193,006

Total: $2,993,350

THOMAS P. DiNAPOLI
Member of Assembly
16th District
Nassau County
Long Island

THE ASSEMBLY
STATE OF NEW YORK
ALBANY

CHAIR
Commission on Solid Waste Management

CHAIR
Task Force on Long Island Sound

CO-CHAIR
Commission on Water Resource
Needs of Long Island

VICE-CHAIR
Commission on Toxic Substances and
Hazardous Wastes

March 31, 1993

Captain Mark S. Phillips
F/V Illusion
P.O. Box 428
Greenport, NY 11944

Dear Captain Phillips:

This is to thank you for the information you sent me regarding New York State representation on the Mid-Atlantic Marine Fisheries Council. As you are aware, the state representatives on the marine fisheries councils are appointed by the governors of each state.

In order to address similar concerns as those you raised in your letter, I have introduced legislation that would provide improved representation and agency responsiveness for New York State's Marine Fisheries Management Program. Please find enclosed a copy of the bill memo for this legislation.

Your interest in protecting and preserving our marine resources is appreciated.

Sincerely,

Thomas P. DiNapoli
Member of Assembly

TPD:mr2
Encl.

DRAFT BILL MEMO (12/30/92)

SENATE   introduced by Senator X

ASSEMBLY   introduced by Assemblyman Thomas P. DiNapoli

AN ACT to amend environmental conservation law in relation to marine fisheries to enhance the state's management program.

PURPOSE
This bill has been designed to comprehensively enhance the state's marine fishery resources management program.

PROVISIONS
The enhancement proposal has five key components. First, it establishes policy standards for marine fisheries regulatory purposes. Second, it revises the Marine Resources Advisory Council to function as a negotiated rule making body within the Department of Environmental Conservation. Third, it recognizes database deficiencies and puts forward a data collection and analysis program. Fourth, it establishes a Marine Resources Management Board Account and fifth, it finances this account through increases in existing commercial fishing fees, the establishment of a wholesale food fish and crustacean dealer and shipper's license.

JUSTIFICATION
Currently, the DEC and the State Legislature share regulatory authority over marine resources. This arrangement may have been satisfactory in the past, but increasing pressures on the state's fisheries are creating the need for a more responsive, flexible, and accessible management structure. The visible decline of many of the state's more important marine fish species evidences the need for the changes in fisheries management put forward in this bill.

Some of the pressures on the fin and shellfish populations in the New York Marine District are: increases in the number of commercial and recreational fishermen, point and non-point source pollution, and loss of habitat. Commercial and recreational marine fisheries constitute a significant portion of New York's economic base. Fisheries are a sustainable resource, and their stability should not be jeopardized, especially in the current economic climate.

The "Findings" section of the bill states: "as implemented in other coastal states, a well designed anticipatory management strategy is largely dependent upon two elements: a thorough, current database of the best available information regarding marine populations, and an independent rulemaking body." Better fisheries data would ensure that New York received its share of allocations in Federal fishery management plans, and would allow improved regulations for fisheries solely within the state's jurisdiction.

The current decision making regime frustrates user groups and appears to lack specific guidelines or a comprehensive approach. Many commercial and recreational fishermen complain of an inability to influence a regulatory process that often promulgates inefficient or ineffective rules. Without a declared state policy on fisheries, and without effective procedures for accessing the regulatory process, user groups consistently doubt the wisdom of new fishery regulations. This doubt fosters an atmosphere which can lead to willful violations of regulations. Although this bill potentially provides some increased funding for marine enforcement through the establishment of minimum fines for violations, no degree of enforcement can substitute for respect of the fishery regulations by the individual users.

Current marine fisheries regulatory procedures in New York need to be based on more accurate biological assessments to resolve disputes between user groups. These deficiencies weaken the effectiveness of the program, the public's confidence in New York's management authority, the compliance rate of user groups, the Legislature's intent in protecting sustainable marine resources, and the stability of our fishery resources.

FISCAL IMPLICATIONS

The increased fees calculated to finance the allocation for the Account specified in the bill are supported by the effected user groups. Historically, negotiated rule making has involved larger up front costs than the traditional method of agency rule making, however, experience has shown that in the long run, these costs are more than recouped due to decreased litigation, increased compliance, and streamlined administrative review procedures. Accordingly, the long term fiscal impact is a decrease in the State's costs to regulate Marine Fisheries. The benefits of a self-sustaining management account are immeasurable to enhancing ongoing regulatory efforts.

EFFECTIVE DATE

This act shall take effect on January 1, 1994 and includes a sunset date of January 1, 1999.

EAST HAMPTON TOWN BAYMEN'S ASSOCIATION, INC.
BOX 498, AMAGANSETT, NEW YORK 11930

August 11, 1993

Larry Cantwell
Fishing Industry Study Group

Dear Larry,

The Baymen's Association respectfully submit the following ideas for consideration, and comment.

New York State increasingly delegates regulatory power over commercial fishing to the DEC. The rationale is that they have the technical ability to respond to federal mandates, and to react to changes in fish stocks, in a more timely and efficient manner than the legislature itself. This regulatory authority is being used by the department to make all encompassing regulations, such as in the Striped Bass law, 11-0303, in which "the department may adopt regulations prescribing possession, transportation, identification and sale ..." and the Bluefish law,13-0340, where the department may adopt measures " including size limits, catch and possession limits, open and closed seasons, restrictions on the manner of taking and landing, restrictions on the amount and type of fishing effort and gear, and requirements relating to transportation, possession and sale...". Such legislation generally stipulates a guideline, such as a fishery management plan of the Mid-Atlantic Fisheries Management Council.

Commercial fishermen are increasingly restricted by a regulatory method that is unaware of how they work, and little concerned with their success. This unfortunate result, in contradiction to the State policies enumerated in the Governor's Task Force on Coastal Resources, is caused by a case of tunnel vision on the part of regulators charged with achieving very specific goals. Federal management plans stress individual species and ignore the interdependencies inherent in "Mixed fish" fisheries. The impact of fishery management decisions are obscured by the need to satisfy one criteria, the federal one, and the lack of perspective engendered by the use of one agency, the DEC, to decide issues with wide ranging effects.

The gap between the state coastal policy, and federal fishery guidelines, has become huge, and the situation is becoming worse. The problem, simply stated, is that the management of individual species, without consideration of larger issues, creates drastic unintended side effects. DEC lacks the ability and the mandate to implement it's regulatory powers in a way that satisfies the wider intent of the State. The problem is systemic, and the solution requires a wider viewpoint, an awareness of multiple issues, and clearly delineated responsibilities.

The Task Force recommends that the state "provide a forum for the participation of representatives of water dependent businesses to discuss with State agencies new State legislation, regulations and programs that may affect the economic strength of the businesses and/or their ability to remain in New York State". The commercial fishing industry needs such a forum where legislation, regulations and programs can be discussed by industry before these actions become state law or are implemented.

The current Marine Resources Advisory Council is not a satisfactory forum because it lacks the proper makeup to provide knowledgeable and representative information on the effect of actions affecting specific gear types or fisheries. The diverse nature of commercial fisheries militates against united representation on both the State and Federal councils, and the representatives of recreational fishermen are placed in the position of deciding highly technical issues for an industry they frequently deride. It is important to remember the Task Force statement that "The State's marine resources are the property of all New Yorkers. For many, the only access they have to these resources is through the consumer purchase of New York harvested fish. In order to continue to allow for the greatest public benefit from the marine resources, fishing, distribution and marketing should be encouraged in New York State".

What is needed is a board composed of commercial fishermen, who are requested to provide technical information on the impact of proposed regulations, as a mandated step in the development of regulations. The feasibility of regulations should be assessed by those impacted in an orderly framework established by legislation. This proposed legislation to amend the Environmental Conservation Law should be added to all sections where regulatory authority over finfish will be in effect. The advantages of specific procedures for the public and the legislature are many and obvious. It will make the process consistent, provide for public and inter-agency input, allow greater oversight by the legislature, and it will generate greater public support for conservation, and the laws required to enhance it.

We suggest that a board be created that has inter-agency support to assess the effect of proposed regulations and their consistency with state policy apart from concerns over an individual species of fish. The board would have the following format, and would be required to comment on all proposed fishery regulations.

Technical Advisory Board

A technical advisory board of commercial fishermen should be established under the auspices of a state agency (DOS) to provide timely and accurate information about the practical ability of proposed fisheries regulations to achieve their desired results. It would be set up for four purposes:

I. assessing the viability of regulations

II. providing alternatives to regulations

III. suggesting ways to implement the recommendations of the Governor's Task Force on Coastal Resources

IV. gathering and disseminating information on fisheries management

The Board would be composed of seven members, one from each classification of five gear type's (trawlers, handliners, gillnetters, seiners, pound trappers), and a representative of the State agency (DOS) and Sea Grant (Cooperative Extension). This board would be notified of the proposed regulations and would determine if such regulations should be reviewed from a technical perspective.

If the regulations were to be reviewed by the board, it would appoint a temporary sub-committee of knowledgeable specialists (gillnetters to review gillnet marking regulations, for example), headed by the appropriate member or members of the larger committee. The State agency would provide meeting space, clerical help, counsel, liaison and staff. The recommendations of the sub-committee would be reviewed by the technical advisory board as a whole, and final recommendations would be sent to DEC for incorporation into the regulatory process.

Currently, DEC does not know if it's regulations are viable or not and it wastes enormous effort on proposals that are unrealistic or ill-designed. The creation of this board would benefit the regulators by providing an incentive for the regulated to participate in the process and share their experience and knowledge. This would result in more efficient and balanced regulations. It would also provide an opportunity for comment on the rationale behind the regulations, and a degree of oversight on the success of the DEC in representing New York State on the federal level. As new management plans are developed, New York has been consistently short changed in it's allocations because of the greater degree of regulation already in place on the State level.

The single goal of our proposal is to ensure that commercial fishing is not ensnared by a succession of well intended regulations that are not measured by their cumulative impact. The flaws in the current regulatory method prevent their success in the context of overall State policy.

Desired Procedure for Fisheries Management:

1. Legislature gives DEC regulatory power over "dogfish".

2. Currently no regulations for the taking of "dogfish" exist.

3. DEC chooses to propose a regulation limiting the take of "dogfish".

4. The DEC and MRAC develop information on the fish and the need for conservation measures.

5 After determining the need for regulations, the process of developing the necessary regulations begins and proposals are made to achieve a specific goal.

6. Their viability is appraised by a technical oversight group (this is where we would want the opportunity to provide information and correct insanities)

7. The extent of the regulation's scope would be assessed (how narrow and focused the regulation is, and what accidental effect it would have.

8. DEC would return regulation to MRAC for approval and would than seek input from agencies and the public as it currently does.

9. Technical advisory group would propose alternative regulations to meet the defined goal.

10. When the proposals are modified, the process loops back to the MRAC and the technical advisory group.

The essential change that we need is the ability to examine regulations before time is too pressing and the momentum of the process demands the passage of inefficient and ill considered regulations. Steps 6 through 8 are what we want, and what we think can work.

These ideas have been developed and discussed by the baymen's mixed fish committee over a two year period, and portions of our proposal have been discussed with several elected officials. We hope that a rational implementation process for fishery regulations can be developed. If you have any questions, please call me at 267-8856.

Sincerely yours,

Thomas E. Knobel
mixed fish committee

Community Appearance and Tourism: *What's The Link?*

By Edward T. McMahon

The colorful brochures American cities and towns use to promote their charms are always filled with attractive scenes: sunsets, azaleas in bloom, historic house museums beautifully photographed. The reality is often not so lovely. Back away from the great columned house and you'll find, as likely as not, a fast food restaurant with screaming red roof to one side, and to the other a parking lot that is barren except for a flashing portable sign and a towering billboard. The brochure is handsome; the city is not.

There is an immense but too often ignored relationship between community appearance and tourism. As Mark Twain once said, "We take stock of a city like we take stock of a man. The clothes or appearance are the externals by which we judge." Unfortunately many tourism officials are far more concerned with marketing and promotion—creating fancy brochures and compellilng ads—than they are with protecting and enhancing the product they are trying to sell.

> To preserve and enhance those characteristics that make a community interesting, memorable, and attractive, the tourism industry should adhere to the following standards and recommendations:
>
> • Identify all of those places, both natural and man-made, that give a community its special character and identity.
>
> • Make every effort to preserve the authentic aspects of local culture including handicrafts, art, music, language, dress, architecture, traditions, and history.
>
> • Preserve and maintain existing historic buildings, neighborhoods, towns and areas.
>
> • Insure that tourism support facilities—hotels, motels, restaurants, and shops—are architecturally compatible with their natural and man-made surroundings.
>
> • Protect the gateways and entryways into a community and identify and protect streets and roads with outstanding scenic or historic significance.
>
> • Protect scenic views and vistas. Wherever possible install underground utility wires and screen unsightly intrusions on scenic viewsheds or historic settings.
>
> • Preserve trees and existing landscape character. Wherever possible plant street trees and use native vegetation to landscape and buffer parking lots.
>
> • Prohibit billboards and strictly limit the size, height and number of other outdoor signs. Encourage the use of natural materials—not plastic—in sign design.

Tourism involves much more than marketing. It also involves making destinations more appealing. This means conserving and enhancing a destination's natural tourism asset. It is, after all, the heritage, culture and natural beauty of a community or region that attracts tourists. But today a person dropped along a road outside of most American cities (whether tourist destination or not) wouldn't know where he was because it all looks the same. Is it Albany or Allentown? Clarksdale or Cowpens? Providence or Pittsburgh? Who can tell?

The truth is, the more a community does to enhance its unique set of assets, whether natural, architectural, or cultural, the more tourists it will attract. On the other hand the more a community comes to resemble Anyplace, U.S.A., the less reason there will be to visit. Make a destination more appealing and people will stay longer and spend more.

Clearly, certain places have more appeal than others. But no place will retain its special appeal by accident. Without exception those places that have successfully protected their uniqueness—whether natural or man-made—are those places that have used vision, management and control to protect the features that make them special. Without planning and management, tourism can destroy the very attributes—both natural and man-made—that people come to see. As a result, local policies that shape growth and development are critical to the success of tourism development efforts.

Many cities have gotten used to ugliness, accepting it as inevitable to progress. But there are others across America who have begun an active push for a more appealing environment. The tools to make a community memorable and beautiful are not new or rare. But it takes citizen action and political will to put these tools to work. It also takes an understanding of how people, particularly tourists, see and experience a community.

Perception studies reveal significant differences between tourist and commuter perceptions of a community from the highway. Tourists are open and receptive to everything they see, while commuters tend to tune out the familiar environment along the roads they travel day in and day out. This suggests that tourism officials need to become more aware of the overall character of a community. This is particularly true because many tourists decide to spend time and money at a location before they actually see the product. If the character of the destination is at odds with its description in advertising and promotional literature, the tourist will feel cheated. Creation of a false image can spoil a vacation. What's more, it can reduce repeat visitation: tourists may come once but they won't come back. Alternatively, happy memories and word of mouth are the best public relations a destination can have.

Tourism is a voluntary activity, which means that tourists have a choice among competing destinations. Given a choice, where will they go? Virtually every study of traveller motivations has shown that, along with rest and recreation, visiting scenic areas and historic sites are among the top two or three reasons why people travel. Travel writer Arthur Frommer says that, "Among cities with no particular recreational appeal, those that have preserved their past continue to enjoy tourism. Those that haven't, receive almost no tourism at all. Tourism simply doesn't go to a city that has lost its soul."

Preservation-minded cities like Victoria, B.C.; Savannah, Ga.; Charleston, S.C.; and Alexandria, Vir., are among North America's leading tourism destinations because they have protected and enhanced their unique architectural heritage. By contrast, cities which have obliterated their past such as Cleveland, Birmingham and Atlanta attract hardly any tourists at all, except for the highly competitive and notorious fickle convention business.

Urban Planner Andreas Duany says that, "Authentic urban experience has become such a rarity that many places have become tourist attractions simply by virtue of being real towns." Visitors drive hundreds of miles to spend a weekend in places like Fredricksburg, Tex.; Madison, Ind.; Sonoma, Calif.; Stockbridge, Mass. and Edenton, N.C., just for the sake of experiencing the pleasures of a "real" small town. Duany also believes this explains the success of Disneyland and Disney World, where visitors spend more time wandering along Main Street USA than they do on rides.

Growth is inevitable. The ugliness and destruction of community character that so often accompanies growth is not. Communities can grow without destroying the things people love. Beauty, heritage, and environmental quality are good for business. Unless the tourist industry thinks it can continue to sell trips to see look-a-like motels, tract housing, traffic jams, and cluttered commercial strips, it ought to share in an agenda to protect the natural and cultural resources on which it relies.

Edward T. McMahon, a Senior Associate at The Conservation Fund, is former president of Scenic America.

APPENDIX L

TECH MEMO

THE ECONOMIC BENEFITS OF LAND CONSERVATION

By Holly L. Thomas, Senior Planner
Dutchess County Planning Department

There is a long-held belief about undeveloped land—that even though it may be nice to look at it's not economically productive, and that it only really carries its weight in the local tax base after it is developed. Communities in growing areas are finding out that this belief is wrong. More and more studies are showing that conserving open land and choosing carefully those areas that should be developed is not contrary to economic health, but essential to it.

The choice we face is not one of environment and aesthetics versus economics, after all. Instead, the fact is that land conservation is a sound investment. Studies comparing the fiscal impacts of development to those of open space protection have found that open space preservation has a more positive impact on a community's economy than most conventional forms of suburban-style development, even when property is preserved through public dollars.

This does not mean that open space protection should be used as an excuse to exclude the diverse housing, schools, roads, businesses, and services needed to keep a community accessible and sound. In fact, providing affordable housing and infrastructure and protecting open space all involve using land appropriately and concentrating development where it can best be served.

What the findings that land conservation is a sound investment do mean is that development is not a sure-fire economic boon and protecting the resource base pays off. Development that destroys community resources and natural features is both economically and environmentally wasteful.

Economic Benefits

The following seven points indicate the range of economic benefits of land conservation.

1. Land conservation is often less expensive for local government than suburban-style development.

The old adage that cows do not send their children to school expresses a documented fact—that farms and other types of open land, far from being a drain on local taxes, actually subsidize local government by generating far more in property taxes than they demand in services.

The opposite is true of most suburban forms of residential development. In other words, maintaining a substantial open space system is one important way of controlling the costs of government.

To cite one example, a recent study of Boulder, Colorado's open space program costs found the following:

Average Annual Public Cost of Maintaining Public Open Space Lands (including debt service on land purchases and administrative costs)	$328/acre
Average Annual Public Cost of Maintaining Developed and Developable Lands	$2,524/acre

Closer to home, a 1990 study of revenues and expenditures for various types of land uses in Red Hook, Fishkill, and Amenia, by Scenic Hudson, Inc. found that residential land required $1.11 to $1.23 in services for every dollar it contributed in revenue, while open land required only $0.17 in services in Amenia, $0.22 in Red Hook, and $0.74 in Fishkill for each one dollar contribution.

A 1989 study by Cornell Cooperative Extension of Dutchess County and the American Farmland Trust found that in Beekman and North East, residential lands required $1.12 to $1.36 for every dollar they contributed, while agricultural land required only $0.21 for every dollar it contributed in North East, and $0.48 for every dollar it contributed in Beekman.

Studies throughout the country are showing similar results. Researchers in Wright County, Minnesota, for example, found that the average annual shortfall between taxes paid and the cost of services required was $490 for developed house lots larger than one acre, and $114 for quarter-acre lots. The extent to which undeveloped land subsidizes development, particularly the kind of large-lot suburban development that consumes more space than it really needs, is beginning to hit home.

The Scenic Hudson and Cooperative Extension studies and others have shown that commercial and industrial land uses also demand less in services than they pay in taxes. However, it is important to remember that commercial and industrial growth encourages residential growth. Working farms do not.

DUTCHESS COUNTY PLANNING DEPARTMENT   FEBRUARY 1991

Although the methods used in the two Dutchess County studies do not address all variables, the magnitude of the differences between the costs of serving agricultural or other undeveloped land and residential developments is striking. Their findings agree with experience; taxes increase as farms turn into suburbs.

2. Giving land conservation a high priority encourages more cost-efficient development.

Clustering involves grouping buildings on parts of a piece of property instead of spreading them out in a way that consumes the entire parcel. The concept of clustering can be applied to single-family detached homes as well as multi-family or townhouse styles and non-residential uses. Clusters are frequently referred to as open space subdivisions because they can be designed to keep the most important undeveloped land on a site—such as productive farm fields or wildlife corridors—intact.

The National Association of Home Builders first documented the economic benefits of clustering in 1976. In evaluating this tool for encouraging development and land conservation at minimal public cost, the association found that a sample 472-unit cluster cost 34% less to develop than a conventional grid subdivision.

These costs vary from site to site, but follow the general principle that well-designed clusters—both high-density clusters in community centers and low-density clusters of detached units in rural areas—consume less land, require shorter roads and pipes, and fit in better with traditional community densities than do the suburban grids and spider-webs that are spreading across our landscape. They also allow for the preservation of natural systems and agricultural resources whose true value cannot be calculated.

When communities make it clear that protecting open space is a high priority and that unsatisfactory designs will not be accepted, developers are encouraged—or required—to find attractive ways to increase the cost-efficiency of their proposals.

Responsible open space protection involves deciding where and how development should occur as well as where it should not. By retaining the most important natural, scenic, historic, recreational, or agricultural assets, it concentrates development where it fits best, and leads to better decisions about how and where tools such as clustering should be used and where investments in roads, water supplies, and sewers should be made.

3. Communities with well thought-out land protection programs may improve their bond ratings.

Bond ratings are measures of the financial community's faith in the ability of a government to meet its obligations and manage its debts. Favorable ratings save governments money by enabling them to raise money for capital improvements at relatively low costs. The poorer the bond rating, the higher the interest the government has to pay to attract investors, and the greater the chance that potential investors will place their money elsewhere.

Bond ratings are beginning to reflect the fact that unlimited or mismanaged growth can threaten a community's fiscal health, while land conservation and sound planning can help sustain it. The rating assigned to Howard County, Maryland, which lies in the rapidly growing Baltimore to Washington, D.C. corridor, is one example. Howard County has one of the most innovative farmland preservation programs in the country. It stretches public dollars by combining installment purchases of development rights with property tax abatements.

In May, 1990, Fitch Investors Service gave the county a AAA bond rating for the issuance of over $55 million in bonds for capital projects because of its record and its specific plans for limiting and managing growth. In its report on the bond issue, Fitch states

> The recently completed general plan for future county development is an example of the county's superior planning skill. A conscious decision has been made after discussions with residents and business, to control future growth within the county to ensure that the quality of life continues to be desirable. Components of the plan include maintaining a rural character in parts of the county, adopting adequate public facilities ordinances to require that infrastructure is in place before permitting development and providing a contribution of funds to ensure that state roads are in a condition necessary to provide adequate transportation access.

The report goes on to state that

> an important and unique part of the capital improvement plan is the agricultural preservation program under which development rights are purchased by the county to control growth and maintain the area's character.

In other words, the development limits the county has put in place, including a farmland preservation program financed by public dollars, enhance the county's fiscal integrity by demonstrating the county's commitment to maintaining the quality of life and controlling the costs of development.

In its presentation to the Fitch Investors Service, the county argued that because its programs limited the amount of land that could be developed, they limited the amount of infrastructure the county would have to provide. This meant that the county would not have to go into as much debt for infrastructure construction, and could more easily carry any other debt it incurred. In awarding the AAA rating, Fitch Investor Service agreed. It acknowledged that rationally limiting growth would be significantly less expensive than allowing growth to continue unconstrained.

The Howard County agricultural development rights purchase program won the Government Finance Officers 1990 national award for innovation in financial management and continues to attract national attention.

4. Open space protection saves public funds by preventing development of hazardous areas.

Floodplains function well as emergency drainage systems—for free—when they are left undisturbed. The public pays a high price when misplaced or poorly designed development interferes with this function. Human encroachment on the natural flood corridors often increases the risk to down-stream homes and businesses by increasing the volume of runoff and altering the flood path. The resulting demands for costly drainage improvements, flood control projects, flood insurance, and disaster relief are all, ironically, preventable by conserving and respecting the floodplains from the outset. Rockland County's greenways acquisition program was inspired by the county's dismay over the costs of coping with drainage problems caused by encroachment into floodplain systems.

5. Conserving land allows nature to continue its valuable work.

Two functions that wetlands provide for free—groundwater recharge and water purification—are lost when those wetlands are developed. Suffolk County's groundwater recharge area acquisition program was triggered by public awareness that uncontrolled growth threatened the quality and quantity of the county's water supply. The county's voters realized that protecting the groundwater system by buying important areas above it made better economic sense than finding another water source.

As noted above, the ability of a natural floodplain to channel floodwaters efficiently—for free—can cause a public emergency when development gets in the way. The remedies needed to protect life and property after floodplains are improperly developed are limited and costly.

Steep slopes are another example of natural systems that operate best when left alone. Woodlands hold fragile soils in place on steep terrain—for free—when they are left undisturbed. Too often when those slopes are cleared for development, their soils erode and clog streams, lakes and drainage ways. Soil is an irreplaceable resource and the cost of dredging streams and lakes is prohibitive.

Wooded slopes also help absorb rain water and slow the rate of stormwater runoff. When too much pavement replaces the vegetation, the costs of preventing more serious and frequent floods and of maintaining water quality skyrocket.

6. Open space increases the value of nearby or adjacent property.

Results of a 1978 study of Boulder, Colorado's greenbelt indicated that property value decreased by $4.20 for every foot of distance from the public open space. More recent studies of greenway corridor paths, park lands and lands under conservation easements throughout the country, in settings ranging from the most urban to rural also found that access to protected open space is a valuable amenity in the real estate market.

7. Outdoor recreation, tourism, and agriculture are big business.

Tourism and agriculture are vital components of Dutchess County's economy, and both depend on the resource amenities that open landscapes provide. According to the 1987 Census of Agriculture, Dutchess County's farmers sold $38 million worth of agricultural products in 1987 and employed 1,500 people on farms and another 2,000 to 2,500 in farm-related goods and services. They spent over $33 million on goods and services, which multiplied to an infusion of over $100 million into our local economy.

Tourism is also a multi-million dollar business in Dutchess County. Statistics from the Dutchess County Tourism Promotion Agency show that tourists spent over $127 million here in 1988, up nine percent from 1987. The agency estimates that this represented an economic benefit to the county of $376.8 million. The tourism business employed over 8,850 persons in 1988, one in every ten of the county's workers.

The county's historic buildings and sites are important tourism attractions. Many of these historic features are linked to natural and scenic settings that are relatively unprotected. Conserving these landscapes would help sustain the appeal of the cultural sites, thereby protecting both their historic integrity and their economic contribution.

Outdoor recreation is a major component of the tourism economy, but also serves the county residents who consider access to parks, Hudson River views, historic sites, fishing streams, forest trails, hunting areas, or rural scenes important elements of the quality of life that drew them here.

Conclusion

The value of a productive farm field, a healthy wetland system, or an irreplaceable scenic vista goes far beyond dollars and cents. It is important, however, that we understand the real economic benefits of protecting open space. As these examples show, the benefits can range from filtering water and channelling floods for free, or avoiding the increased costs of serving homes arranged in sprawling grids, to attracting tourist dollars to the region, or influencing the bond ratings that govern the costs of long-term debt.

Too often our communities are presented with a false choice between economic growth and environmental protection. Success in attaining and sustaining economic health depends on recognizing the economic contribution that undeveloped land already makes.

> In choosing which areas should develop, and how, we owe it to ourselves and to our heirs to ensure that important natural systems and our most productive landscapes remain intact. We should also provide for development that will meet community needs for housing, jobs, recreation, and services, and insist that such development respects and complements the values of open lands. By following these principles we can join the growing number of communities throughout the country that have found that a public commitment to combining land stewardship with well-designed development pays off.

References

Note: Many of the concepts included here were presented in 1979 by the New Jersey Conservation Foundation, in *Open Space Pays: The Socioenvironomics of Open Space Preservation*. The following sources were used to update, augment, and amend the 1979 information to reflect current knowledge and facts relevant to Dutchess County.

American Farmland Trust, *Density-Related Public Costs*, Washington, DC: 1966

Arendt, Randall, "Patterns in the Rural Landscape." Orion Nature Quarterly, pp. 24-27, Autumn 1989.

Bucknell, Christopher P. *The Real Cost of Development*, Poughkeepsie, NY: Scenic Hudson, Inc., 1990

Caputo, Darryl F. *Open Space Pays: The Socioenvironomics of Open Space Preservation*, Morristown, NJ: New Jersey Conservation Foundation, 1979

Cornell Cooperative Extension of Dutchess County and American Farmland Trust. *Cost of Community Services Study: Towns of Beekman and Northeast Dutchess County, New York*, Millbrook, NY: 1989.

Cornell, Mark R., Jane H. Lilydahl, and Larry D. Singell, "The Effects of Greenbelts on Residential Property Values: Some Findings on the Political Economy of Open Space." Land Economics, Vol. 54: pp. 204-217, 1976.

Crain, James C., correspondence with Albert Bartlett, "Revised Estimated Costs to Maintain Open Space Versus Developed, Annexed Land." Boulder, CO: Department of Real Estate/Open Space, City of Boulder, Nov. 2, 1988.

Fitch Investor Services, Inc. "Public Finance-Tax Supported New Issue, Howard County, Maryland." New York, NY: May 22, 1990.

Fox, Tom. *Urban Open Space: An Investment That Pays—Real Estate Values*, New York, NY: The Neighborhood Open Space Coalition, 1990.

Frank, James E. *The Costs of Alternative Development Patterns: A Review of The Literature*, Washington, DC: The Urban Land Institute, 1989.

Land Design Research, Inc. *Cost-Effective Site Planning*. Washington, D.C. The National Association of Home Builders, 1976.

Peters, James E. "Saving Farmland: How Well Have We Done?" Planning, Vol. 56 No. 9, pp. 12-17, September 1990.

Regional Plan Association, *Greenspaces and Greenways: 1. The Open Space Imperative*, New York, NY: 1987.

Yard, Robert D., Randall G. Arend, Harry L. Dodson, and Elizabeth A. Brabese. *Dealing with Change in the Connecticut River Valley: A Design Manual for Conservation and Development*, Amherst, MA: Center for Rural Massachusetts, University of Massachusetts at Amherst, 1988.

27 HIGH STREET • POUGHKEEPSIE • NEW YORK • 12601 • AC (914) 485-9681

Goodwill Games Should Swim East

By Steven T. Kenny

The excitement over the great news that the New York-New Jersey region has been chosen to play host to the 1998 Goodwill Games is tempered by the disappointment that eastern Suffolk was overlooked as one site for the games. At a time when eastern Long Island is locked in a struggle to define its economic future—involvoing the proposed jetport at Calverton—the Goodwill Games offer an opportunity that perfectly suits the existing economic base of the area.

The games require at least one capital project for facilities to accommodate the athletic events. Gov. Mario Cuomo has pledged $4 million to build a center for the swimming and diving.

The plan to construct an aquatics center near Hofstra University is a wasteful investment of public funds. Mitchel Field already houses two pool complexes: the 50-meter Hofstra pool and the 25-yard Nassau Community College pool and diving tank. These two excellent facilities augment an array of public pools dotting Nassau and western Suffolk. A third swimming complex in the vicinity yields small extra value to the swimming public and only a temporary boost to the economy of Nassau. Simply put, the proposed center is a duplication of existing facilities and offers little long-term economic benefit to the immediate area. And it is not too late to reverse the site decision.

A significant public purpose would be gained if an aquatic center were put on eastern Long Island. About an hour's drive from the Mitchel Field site, an aquatics center on the East End would spread the Goodwill Games to venues throughout Long Island, sharing the tourism dollars from the event with Suffolk hotels and welcoming visitors to the most rural and beautiful part of the Island. If tourism promotion is one of the goals of the organizers, the jewel of the metropolitan area's tourism industry is missing from this setting.

Relocating the swimming events to eastern Long Island disperses venues, but the distances and travel are in keeping with last summer's Olympics in Spain. Moving the swimming competition to the East End would promote an important tourism region for New York. The real profit, however, will be in the facilities left for the public and the economy of the East End when the Goodwill Games are over.

Establishing an aquatics center would create a sorely needed, public recreational facility for a rural community that has no enclosed public pool. After the Goodwill Games, this center could be used by school districts to teach swimming to children and to train students in life-saving techniques for seasonal life-guarding jobs at our beaches. It is one of the ironies of residing on the East End that public swimming-instruction programs, common all over the state, are nonexistent in our water-surrounded community.

The aquatics center would extend the season for tourism. Second-home owners would have a reason to spend winter weekends here. U.S. Swimming Association meets would attract the families of competitors to fill hotels and motels during off-season weekends. It could also be developed as a training facility, similar to Lake Placid, for regional Olympic swimming and diving hopefuls.

The funding for this aquatics center would also be more cost-effective. New York State and Suffolk County commitments to complete the Suffolk Community College Campus in Riverhead, now without physical-education facilities, could be accelerated and tailored for this purpose.

The college could agree to forgo the standard plan for a gymnasium, athletic fields, a track and a pool at this campus, and opt for this specialized sports center. Instead of industrializing the East End with a jetport, invest in "recreationalizing" it. An aquatics center, ice-skating rinks, bicycle paths, hiking trails, bridle paths, parks and other outdoor and recreational facilities could open eastern Long Island to all-season recreation and nature tourism. This strategy is far more compatible with the culture, communities and environment of eastern Long Island than developing the Grumman Airport at Calverton.

The rural setting, open spaces, and small towns and villages of the East End are treasures for all Long Island and New York State residents to enjoy. The 1998 games are still far enough away that our area could be included. Spread the Goodwill Games to eastern Long Island.

Steven T. Kenny is chairman of the Southampton Town Planning Board and provost of Suffolk Community College, eastern campus.

1993 I Love New York Program

A. Advertising:

1. Upstate Summer Campaign
   Media
   - Magazines — $739,100
   - Newspapers — 159,800
   - Carol Wright (Direct Mail) — 99,900

Subtotal Media	$ 998,800
Production	$ 176,200
Great Lakes Program	$ 25,000

   Total Upstate Summer Campaign — **$1,200,000**

2. New York City Campaign
   Media
   - Magazines — $769,500
   - Newspapers — 85,500

Subtotal Media	$ 855,000
Production	$ 45,000

   Total New York City Campaign — $ 900,000
3. Other Campaigns — $ 250,000
4. Research — $ 50,000

   Subtotal Advertising — **$2,400,000**

B. Marketing:

1. Collateral Distribution — $ 300,000
2. "800" Number Service — $ 289,000
3. Trade/Consumer Shows — $ 9,000
4. Trade Education — $ 2,000

   Subtotal Marketing — $ 600,000

   TOTAL 1992-93 I Love New York Program — **$3,000,000**

DETAILED PLAN FOR THE PRESERVATION OF THE EAST END MARITIME HERITAGE & RESTORATION OF GREENPORT'S DEEP-WATER HARBOR FACILITIES

Background:

MARITIME AND SHIPBUILDING HERITAGE—More than 550 vessels were constructed on the East End between 1830 and 1950, from offshore schooners to three-masted barkentines, from patrol boats to minesweepers. Local boatbuilder Frederick C. Beebe designed and manufactured a self-bailing, self-righting lifeboat, which was used exclusively for many years by the U.S. Life Saving Service. Both Sag Harbor and Greenport was noted for being whaling ports. Over 200 whaling ships left the East End from 1795 to the mid-1800's on whaling expeditions, and their successes were an important part of the East End economy and its maritime heritage.

AMERICA'S CUP—The East End of Long Island was noted for its participation in the defense of the America's Cup, especially during the era of the J-Boats, considered the most spectacular of all of the America's Cup vessels. All three of the America's Cup defenders during this era were captained by Greenport resident, Captain George Monsell, and were crewed primarily by East Enders.

THE SPARK—The only United States Navy sailing vessel built on Eastern Long Island was the *Spark*, built in 1813 in Sag Harbor. This was not just any ship, but was part of Commodore Stephen Decatur's squadron, who successfully carried out operations against the pirates of Algiers who were enslaving American seamen. She was also used as a presidential courier ship because it was considered the fastest ship the Navy had during that period and also distinguished itself in stopping pirate activities in the Caribbean.

THE PICKET PATROL—During World War II, the Navy and Coast Guard, in desperation to reduce shipping losses from U-Boats, recruited private yacht and sailboat owners to serve as a Coast Guard Auxiliary to observe and report on German submarine movements and to rescue survivors of torpedoed ships. Based in Greenport, the Picket Patrol, also known as the Hooligan Navy or the Canvas Hangers, are a unique chapter in the heroism, hardship, and dedication of East Enders.

AMERICA'S SAIL '95—A large group of historic Tall Ships, mainly from South America, are racing from the Southern United States to Montauk point in June of 1995. After the race, they are available to be hosted in local deep-water ports. Greenport, with its dockside water depths is one of the few locations that can accommodate these large vessels.

TALL SHIP SERVICING—More and more countries, provinces, and states are building Tall Ships, especially for youth training programs, but there is a serious lack of shoreside facilities that has the capability and support services and people that can perform major repair and maintenance. Greenport, the East End's principal seaport, is a veritable microcosm of ships and maritime services, most within walking distance of the docks. In a recent questionnaire sent to American Sail Training Association members, sixteen ships have given written indication of interest to come to Greenport for their maintenance and repair work from as far away as Vancouver, British Columbia. In response to this, rehabilitation of a section of the waterfront and shipyard facilities needs to be accomplished.

VISITING TALL SHIPS—Because of the available ship services, its unique maritime character, and the Barkentine *Regina Maris* dockside, Greenport has become an increased attraction for visiting Tall Ships from all over the world. For example, the *Georg Stage* from Copenhagen came to Greenport last year as its official port of entry into the United States and attracted over three thousand visitors, making it a major tourist attraction.

RECOMMENDATIONS:

1. Develop a comprehensive detailed plan to promote Greenport's deep-water port as an attraction to Tall Ships and tie that into their unique tourist attraction.

2. Have State support for the restoration of the former 600-ton Marine Railway (ISTEA Proposal of 1993 and 1994).

3. Promote plans to further restore the *Regina Maris* as a dockside, historic, museum-type attraction in recognition of Dr. George Nichols, famed ocean-racer and founder and principal of the Ocean Research Education Society, which was responsible for the whale research that resulted in the present-day international control over their preservation.

4. Continue to promote and support the new East End Seaport Maritime Museum as a repository for the East End's maritime heritage and for an educational entity of the East End's past and present maritime activities.

5. Coordinate all of the above maritime activities into an organized tourist attraction to include Harborwalks, public access areas, and so forth.

6. Have B.O.C.E.S. develop an apprenticeship program for the maintenance and continuation of the fast-becoming-extinct, unique trade to maintain and service replica vessels to include rigging, blacksmithing, and so forth.

7. Develop plans for having a Youth Sail Training Ship built and operated out of the East End for the youth of Long Island and New York State, such as a replica of the *Spark*. In this era of troubled youth, other countries, provinces, and the states are recognizing that the sea can mature and strengthen a young person as no other environment on earth. The sea can be nurturing and calming or a fury to be reckoned with. The young person who learns to cope with this most powerful of nature's forces also learns to cope with the forces and furies within. Massachusetts has the *Ernestina*; Rhode Island has the *Providence*; Texas has the *Elsia*; Maine has the *Discovery*; California has the *Californian*; Pennsylvania has the *Bill of Rights*; etc. Long Island and New York State should seriously consider this proven method of youth problem prevention and changing their direction by teaching character education and values.

The following proposals would enable the railroad museum to reach some short-term goals identified by the museum trustees and would assist in the further development of the tourist industry on the eastern end of Long Island.

1) *Real Property Acquisition*—The railroad museum currently has an agreement with the MTA/L.I.R.R. to store the current equipment collection outdoors at Riverhead.

With the acquisition of real property, the museum would be able to erect in the future a building to protect the equipment collection and to offer tours year-round to visitors.

2) *Mechanical evaluation of Steam Locomotive #39*
   Projected cost $5,000

3) *Purchase a new Steam Locomotive*—Steam locomotives are still produced overseas. With a new locomotive, the railroad museum would be able to generate sufficient revenue for proposals 1-2. Assistance from the L.I.R.R. for the safe operation of any equipment over the railroad would be needed also. Projected cost—under $500,000.

4) *The total rebuilding of historic diesel locomotive Ex-LIRR 1556.*

The railroad museum currently stores this locomotive at a private siting in Riverhead.

This summer, the LIRR mechanical department did a detailed evaluation of the locomotive: Projected cost—$1,300,000.

5) *The rebuilding of baggage-mail car 7737.*

The baggage-mail car is one of the most recent contributions from the LIRR and has been under restoration. The railroad museum would allow the LIRR use for a bicycle storage car for visitors enroute to eastern Long Island. No cost projections at this time.

6) *Heating and climate control.*

The railroad museum currenty is a seasonal operation at the circa 1890 freight station in Greenport. A heating plan would enable the museum to operate year-round at Greenport. Projected cost is under $10,000.

STATE OWNERSHIP OF LAND IN THE FIVE EAST END TOWNS

		Acreage
1	Accabonac Wetlands	7
2	Barcelona Neck State Park	341
3	David Sarnoff Preserve	2,056
4	Hallock Bay	112
5	Hither Hills State Park	1,755
6	Hither Woods (north)	560
7	Laurel Lake	13
8	Little Bay	89
9	Mattituck Park	28
10	Montauk Downs State Park	171
11	Montauk Point State Park	1,100
12	Napeague State Park	1,400
13	Northwest Landing conservation area	49
14	Orient Point	1,168
15	Peter's Neck	15
16	Shelter Island Wetlands	39
17	Shinnecock Bay Wetlands (approx.)	50
20	Westhampton Moneybogue Bay	34
		8,987